S0-BCO-080

DESTINY

DESTINY

By
Rose Toren

Shengold Publishers, Inc.
New York

ISBN 0-88400-151-2
Library of Congress Catalog Card Number: 91-060449
Copyright © 1991 by Rose Toren

All rights reserved.
Shengold Publishers, Inc.
18 West 45th Street, New York, NY 10036

Printed in the United States of America

Contents

For my husband Jack,
my daughter Lili and son-in-law Jon,
and my grandson Andrew,
with all my love.

Preface

Why did I write this book? Yes, there is a reason. Did you know that some people, even educated people who should know better, claim that there never was a Holocaust in the first half of the 20th Century?

For a long time this story has been inside me, crying to get out. Obviously, a lot of it is shocking to today's younger generation, but I think it's important for them to know what can happen when hatred and inhumanity become a way of life. I want to forgive the people who did what they did to me in the Holocaust—forgive, but not forget.

Most of all, I'm writing this for my daughter, Lili, so that she may better understand what I lived through when I was a girl. It's also for the others, for my brother and sisters, and for my parents who were murdered by the Nazis. And yes, I write also for myself, to close this terrible chapter of my life.

My story is called *Destiny*, because I am convinced that something has been driving me at every point in my life, driving me to survive and to make people understand what happened in the Holocaust.

Rose Toren
Los Angeles, California
1991

CHAPTER ONE

Return

*Warsaw in 1985 was like a city that was complete-
ly new to me. It had been totally rebuilt since I saw it
last, shortly after World War II when it was in ruins
and rubble. Now the capital of a Communist country,
it was modern and beautiful. Our hotel was as splen-
did as any in Paris or New York, or even in Beverly
Hills which is now my home.*

*My husband, Jack, who had graduated from the
Warsaw Polytechnic Institute, knew the city well. But
looking at it now, he hardly recognized a single
building. Of course the old Jewish Quarter had dis-
appeared. We found only one tiny synagogue, rebuilt
and hidden away in a corner of a block, and what
was left of the Jewish Cemetery. Nothing remained of
the infamous Warsaw Ghetto where inmates, when
they finally realized what "resettlement in the east"
really meant, had risen up in hopeless defiance of the
Nazi occupiers.*

*Warsaw however was not where I came from. We
were here to visit the places where I was born and
had grown up and seen my family taken away, where
I myself had survived the work camps and the horrors. Warsaw was to be our headquarters. Jack and I*

The only remaining synagogue in Warsaw,
Nozyk, reconstructed after the war.

had rented a car with a driver, and would travel from here to the various parts of Poland that had figured in my life story.

I had waited a very long time to come here. But now that I was in Poland, I was afraid of what I would see and what it would do to me. Tension came over me as we set out through the Polish countryside. We would start in Lublin, the largest city in the department of eastern Poland, near my birthplace, a village called Strzyzow.

In the 1920's and 1930's, Strzyzow was a typical "shtetl," a little Jewish village of the kind that was typical of Eastern Europe. It was a short distance by foot or horsedrawn wagon from the larger town of Hrubieszow, and close by the River Bug ("Bougk") in what was then central Poland. Now it is only less than a mile from the Soviet border. My family had lived in the region for too many generations to count, although we had heard talk of a paternal great-grandmother who had come from Vienna.

My parents, Leah and Isaac Orenstein, had been married as teenagers, as was the custom in this kind of community, but in a sharp break from custom, theirs had not been an arranged marriage. An arrangement had been made for Leah, but she and Isaac had other ideas. Isaac threatened that there would be "grave consequences" if the arrangement was carried out. Who knows what he really would have done, but the two sets of parents gave in to youthful determination, and the couple were permitted to marry.

I remember the little low houses with fences around them, a cow or two, lovingly tended vegetable patches, lush orchards of apples and pears, and flower gardens to brighten peoples' lives. An occasional auto or truck passed through, but most carriages were horse-drawn, and I vividly recall the smell of a horse, hot and sleepy, flicking away flies with its tail, making its harness creak and jingle.

There was a tall Christian church in the center of the town, where in passing one caught glimpses of gilt, and images of all kinds of flickering candles and an occasional black-clad priest or nun. But there was no synagogue, even for 60 families. Our services were conducted in a private house, men crowded to one side, women to the other, cantor and rabbi to the fore, hovering over the sacred scrolls.

Of course, we were Jews. There were always the slogans, the names, and the taunts. "Dirty Jews," "Christ killers," and more. These abuses were a given, part of the landscape. But most of the time Christian and Jew lived near each other in an uneasy peace. Their feelings were not usually directed at individual persons. They didn't hate Rosalia Orenstein, they hated Jews.

I was the first child, born in 1923 when Leah was not yet 17. After me came three more girls in quick succession: Rivka, Ida, and Dora. Then in 1933 came the long-awaited baby boy, David. All of us were delivered at home by a local "wojciechowski," a combination doctor, midwife, and nurse practitioner. He was a fine man, well respected in both the Jewish and the Gentile communities, and a good friend of my father's. After David, the fifth child, there was a miscarriage, and then there were no more children.

My grandmother, Isaac's mother, lived with us. She came from a very Orthodox background. Several of her brothers were rabbis or "schochets," ritual slaughterers in the area. They were a good class of people, well-spoken and well-educated.

The marriage of Leah and Isaac proved a good one, a happy marriage for them both. They worked together in their store, while Grandmother kept house. Leah told me that she preferred it that way, that she would have been bored being just a housewife.

Grandmother kept the house kosher. She did all our cooking and baking. The house always smelled of fresh bread baking, a smell that reminded me of summer.

We also made all our butter and cheeses from the milk provided by our cows. The first thing was to churn it with an old-fashioned wooden milk churn. Later we got a more modern centrifugal separator which was still cranked by hand, but it was more efficient. We stored the butter and cheese in a below-ground cold cellar, near the kitchen pantry. Household chores were not a pleasure to me, but I didn't mind going down to the cellar for milk, butter, or cheese. Even on the hottest summer day, the cellar was cool, clean, and fresh.

My sister Rivka, the next oldest after me, and I shared one bedroom. Ida, Dora, and David shared a second bedroom, my parents had a third, and Grandmother had a fourth room all to herself. I felt it was a sign a respect for her, one she well deserved.

On weekends, my grandmother and mother would prepare a special Sabbath dinner together. A few extra places would always be set for any of the poorer Jews in town to come and share our table. The places were seldom empty. Friday evenings became a holiday, a feast, a celebration of family and community, a time of survival and even of comfort.

How well I remember those Fridays. All that baking, cooking, and cleaning. Grandmother had one and sometimes two helpers. They were Christian girls who would come to help her prepare all the meals for Friday night and Saturday.

Sometimes I close my eyes and see the family in their best clothes, gathered around the Sabbath table, Mother lighting and blessing candles, praying for health and prosperity. How I loved that flickering light reflected in the nicely polished silver candlesticks.

The table was always covered with a snow-white cloth and decorated with flowers. We waited for Father, who used to come home from "shtibel," the house used for worship, and bless all us children. Then we sang traditional Sabbath songs, and after that, the meal started.

Grandmother was a very religious woman who wore a wig. Thanks to her, our Sabbath eves were filled with an unforgettable spirit. I remember her explaining to me the frequent presence of one or two strangers at our table. "He is a good man," she used to say. "He does not have money, and that is why we invited him to spend this Sabbath night with us."

Our home was filled with love, respect, and understanding. It was a really warm family home. I know of too few such homes these days.

Our house was right next to the store, and behind them both was our farm property, mostly a vegetable garden and a few animals, dogs, horses, chickens, and cows, tended by hired Polish help. We children all liked to help too—after a fashion.

The house was always cozy and primitive, but clean. I liked it that way. The floors were painted dark red. They were waxed and re-waxed to a bright polish. In my early childhood, the house was lighted only by candles and kerosene lamps. I always loved to watch their flickering reflections in the deep gloss of the polished wooden floors. Later on, just before I left home, we got electricity. Ours was one of the first houses in Strzyzow to get it. I was very proud. And yet I missed the candles and lamps. The light bulbs were easier to read by, but they weren't as pretty.

The house itself was white, inside and out, with heavy dark wood furniture. The kitchen had a large wood-burning stove, massive in its black cast iron, with an oven for baking bread built into the brickwork of the chimney behind it. A collector on the side provided hot water for dishes and washing. Heat for the house also came from the kitchen stove, which we opened to let the heat circulate. In the winter at night, all of us children would sit in the kitchen doing our homework, our feet up toward the stove, until bedtime and often long past. We liked being warm.

When I was very young, our bathroom was an outhouse. Then the village ran plumbing lines from the Bug to the main water tower, which supplied water by gravity to several of the more modern houses. We got a real inside bathroom with a pullchain toilet, and a porcelain bathtub with little claw feet, but no running hot water. We had to pour the hot water into it from the stove collectors, or if there was a lot of demand, from big pots boiling on the range. We took a bath every day, except in the summer when the children were allowed to bathe in the Bug instead.

Our days started with a breakfast that Grandmother prepared. Usually it was a mixture of fried eggs and flour, with a little salt and sugar thrown in. I hated it, but Grandmother wouldn't let me out of the house until I had eaten something, so I ate the flour and egg mixture and complained.

I would take a packed lunch to eat at school. It was usually a meat or egg sandwich, with home-made bread, fresh butter, white cheese, pears or apples from the orchards, and maybe some store candy.

At night, we had soup with almost every meal, potato soup, milk soup, meat soup, vegetable soup, mushroom soup, all home-made. Chicken, roasts, flanken, and on the dairy days, blintzes, latkes, or fish. My favorite meal was little spring chickens with new potatoes, covered with margarine and parsley. I would have preferred butter, but of course that wasn't kosher.

My favorite dessert was raspberries. With lots of kids and not too many raspberries, that could be a problem. It was sometimes solved by Grandmother, who would hide some berries away for me until I was alone with her in the kitchen. I was the first child, and I guess I was always her favorite.

I remember the Bug, our beloved river, a beautiful stream with trees reflecting from its clear water. We bathed there in summer, and men fished or boated through most of the year. It was not navigable in our area. In some places we could ford it on foot, so there were no ugly tugs or barges to smoke up the air or dirty the water. Today it is part of the border between Poland the Soviet Union, but then it was just a beautiful rural river in east-central Poland.

I liked to swim in the river, play with the dogs, and especially to ride the horses. I loved to climb the apple trees in the orchards behind the house. But most of all, I liked to read, sitting outside during the day, and in the kitchen near the stove at night. I read and spoke Polish fluently, as well as any Polish boy or girl, and maybe better. Poles made fun of the Jews for the way they looked, acted, dressed, and talked. But not of me, Rosalia. I made sure that I looked and acted and spoke as well as any of them.

A special friend of mine in Strzyzow was a little deaf Jewish girl named Perla, or "little Pearl." She went to school with me and spoke awkwardly because of her deafness, but I could communicate with her by a sign language that we had taught each other. She always had trouble pronouncing my name, so she found a way to do it without words. I had a little dimple in my chin then, so Perla would point to her own chin when she wanted to say "Rose." I was "The Dimple." In Polish, my name is actually Rosalia. In Hebrew, it is Shoshana, "Rose."

Despite the anti-Semitic atmosphere in Poland at that time, I had a lot of friends in Strzyzow, both Polish and Jewish. We all tried to get along. You never forgot you were a Jew—they never let you—but you could live a decent life.

There were both Polish and Jewish children in my local school. Public school ran from the first through the seventh grade. There were about 30 Jewish and Gentile boys and girls in each class, sitting together on long hard wooden benches. Discrimination and separation were not there yet.

Although I was quiet, I was always good in school. When someone didn't know the answer, even if he was a grade or two above me, the teacher would often call on me, especially in mathematics. The teacher would tell the older students, "Look at Rosalia! She is younger than you, and she knows all the answers." Part of me cringed at being used by her to shame the others, but the other part of me flushed with pride.

I remember my teachers as good, conscientious people, both the men and the women, most of them young. But no Jews, of course.

There weren't too many of the local boys I liked. I wanted something more out of life, like the romance and adventure that I read about in my books. There was one boy in town I did really like, but he was a lot older, maybe 20, while I was only 12 or 13. His name was Mori. He was blonde and blue-eyed, tall, handsome, and very Aryan-looking, although he was Jewish. Mori was a student at a university, and didn't pay much attention to me.

Then one day he came and spoke to my Mother. I sneaked down and overheard them talking. He told her he thought I was a real beauty, and that even when I got older, I would always be beautiful. At that moment I would have died happy. Mori thought I was beautiful.

When I was 8, Mother had decided that it was time to tell me some of the facts of life. So she spinned the yarn about how the stork brought babies. There really were storks in that part of Poland in those days, building huge stick nests on the roofs of buildings, so the story didn't seem too improbable. I prayed that night that the storks would stay away from our house altogether.

When I got my first period, the stork story wasn't good enough any more. It was too hard to talk to Mother about it, but I had a friend named Leah, the same name as my mother, who had already told me about periods, the blood and pain. I had thought she was crazy, but now I realized she must have known something. So I went to her for the rest of the story.

She knew everything all right. At first, I thought she was lying, but I began to see that she made more sense than the stork story.

Christmas in Strzyzow. Yes, I remember Christmas. I loved to decorate the trees in the houses of my Polish girlfriends. Everything was hand-made. Paper cutouts of Saint Nicholas and the angels, painted in bright colors with cotton balls stuck on them. Cookies fresh baked from the ovens, and hand-blown glass ornaments. Candles lighted on the trees, all covered with hand-made tinsel. Truly, a feast for the senses.

It was natural for children, regardless of the religions of their parents, to meet and play together, to participate in family or religious festivals. I could also invite some of my Christian friends to celebrate Chanukah with us.

Now I think that as much as the adults enjoyed the celebrations, we children found them especially wonderful, almost like magic. We lived in a small community together, separated only when our religion imposed that on us. In everyday life, all the inhabitants of Strzyzow, Jews, Poles, and Ukrainians could work and live together fairly peacefully.

During winter, after a big dinner, we youngsters would often go out for a sleigh ride, driven by my father, my uncle, or an older child. I loved everything about sleigh rides—thick mufflers and gloves and boots, six of us on a horse-drawn sleigh, the sounds of bells in the crisp clean air, the horses' hooves ploshing in the snow, joining in the carol singing—for I knew them all—while breathing in the snowy landscape.

The greatest fun we had, however, was sliding down the hills. I could spend hours like that, running up the hills, throwing snowballs at my friends, laughing, while the swift sleigh was going down the sloppy hill. The snow was glittering in the sun, sparkling like small stars of blue, pink, and white. The thick layer of fluffy snow was crunching under our feet. For as far as I could see, the trees were decorated like the Christmas trees in my friends' homes. And although there were no lights or toys on them, it was hard to believe that it was all real. It was more like a landscape painted by an artist to illustrate a book of fairy tales. It looked so clean, so festive.

CHAPTER TWO

Lublin

I loved the frosty, snowy Polish winters. When it was very cold, I could also skate on the Bug. It was frozen for no more than one or two months, but then we could even cross it and reach the other bank. It was of course a natural skating rink, and I loved skating so much that I would look around then and think, "The whole world belongs to me. It is so beautiful and it all belongs to me."

Here in this swift car, driven down a road between Warsaw and Lublin, it was hard to imagine that village child and my state of mind then. And yet the pictures in my memory are so clear. I was telling my husband all I could remember from those days. It was like describing pictures I had once seen and was trying to recall with pain and sorrow.

The driver seldom commented on my stories. I guess he felt sorry for me. When I started to complain of a strong headache, he said, "Rose, if you don't stop, you will not survive this journey."

It was a May night. My journey back to Poland, to all the places where I had grown up, where I had been so happy, and then had suffered so terribly, was like reliving all that had remained silent for so many years, very deep somewhere at the bottom of my heart.

Now again I was in Poland in winter. The countryside looked unreal, like in a dream. It resembled so much the winters of my childhood, the fields and trees covered with a thick coating of snow, everything so quiet and clean. I kept looking out the window and felt as if I were in paradise. That was the outside.

Inside, I suffered terribly. All the wounds opened again, and my head throbbed with pain. We were passing small towns and villages that looked familiar, yet different and strange. Everything was changed. Then we stopped at a small inn in a town somewhere far out in the country. I needed something hot to drink, and the food supplies we had taken with us were nearly finished.

The inn was full. Many young people occupied nearly all the tables. Probably they knew who I was, that I was a stranger, an American tourist, but they were too busy drinking vodka and enjoying themselves to bother us.

We finished our snack and continued on our journey. I wanted to buy flowers and place them on my father's grave. We stopped at the stand where an elderly woman was selling them. She asked me a lot of questions, but I didn't want to tell her who I was and why I had come here.

Suddenly my heart sank. Again as in the days of war, I felt fear, an overwhelming fear that once I was discovered, something bad would happen, that I would be killed or arrested.

I left quickly, paying for the bunch of flowers.

The high school I attended in Lublin, revisited in 1985.

Fear continued to run through me, that awful fear that had accompanied me during all those terrible years. And again I asked myself the same question. "Why did it happen?" I looked around and only then did I notice how empty it was everywhere. There were no more Jews.

We continued on our way back to Strzyzow. As we came closer and closer to Lublin, I wondered what I would find in that region now.

Mother had known all along that I shouldn't raise my hopes too high about going to high school. I was 13 years old, well read, and had had almost perfect grades all along. But there was a lot more to it than that.

For one thing, there was the examination given every summer in Hrubieszow, the one that in theory decided who would go to the State high school there, and who would not. At that time in Poland, State high school education was free, but it was not for everyone. You had to pass an admission examination, and if you were a Jew, you were limited by the official quota.

Both Mother and Father walked to Hrubieszow with me when I went to take the examination. I did well, passing it with high marks, but there was still "the quota," a part of Polish life from the time of Sholem Aleichem and before. From what I heard, the quota was shrinking further, becoming even more restricted.

The high school at Hrubieszow accepted only one or two Jews a year. They were chosen by their grades in the competitive exam, and by some combination of pull and payoffs. I had done well in all the competitions, much better than most of the Polish children who would enter. But when the names of admittees were announced, mine was not among them.

I was heartbroken. My mother had warned me that my chances were small. She had taken me aside and told me that if I didn't get in the first time, I could stay at home and read, or work in the store and take the exam again the next year. Or maybe I would meet someone, she said. There are other things in life besides high school.

But not for me, however, not then. I wanted to go to high school, and go that year, if not in Hrubieszow, then someplace else. Lublin was a big city, the closest one to Strzyzow, and an important center for Jewish life. It had lots of high schools. Why not there? Lublin was four or five hours away by bus or train. To go to school in the city, I would have to live there. And that, said Mother, was most certainly out of the question.

It wasn't just the money for school, or the cost of the room and board. There would have to be a private school that would take Jews. And who would look after me? I was far too young to be on my own in a strange city. It was simply impossible. Still, my mind was made up.

I was determined to go, and the more Mother resisted, the more I wanted it. Finally I said I was going to starve myself until she relented. I remember that Mother smiled. "Rose, not eat? I don't think so."

But I didn't eat all that day, or the next. Grandmother looked at Mother. Mother looked at Father. Father looked at the ceiling. I continued my hunger strike, although I had a little help from Grandmother when nobody was looking.

After two or three days, they started to give in, at least a bit. They would think about it. Mother recalled that she had a cousin in Lublin, only she couldn't remember her address or even her name. She had married, and it was different now, but if she should see her cousin or her husband, maybe they could help us.

Father smiled. Lublin was a city of over 100,000 people. How could Mother expect to find her cousin? I certainly didn't know either, but it sounded like progress. I was ready to go and try. What did I have to lose? But if we were going to Lublin, we both had to be properly dressed.

"Mother, I want you to look like a real lady," I told her, and she nodded. "Why not?" So we went to Hrubieszow to buy a hat. If we were going to Lublin, she had to have a proper hat. We found two, in fact, one for Mother and one for me, big plumy things, quite the fashion in those days. They were a big hit, the hats, and we wore them the next day as Poppa drove us down in the carriage to the bus station, from which we would set out for Lublin. I think we both looked very pretty.

It was the summer of 1936, and I was 13 years old. The road was leading to what I knew would be a grand adventure, a bright and exciting future. The ride to Lublin was beautiful. We left very early, just as the sun was rising. I remember the trees, the flowers, the excitement. Never until that day had I been farther away from home than Hrubieszow.

We got to Lublin in mid-afternoon. So far we hadn't figured out how to locate this mysterious cousin, but at least we were all in the same city. We hoped maybe the local Jewish agencies would help. Mother thought her cousin was fairly wealthy and would be known in the community.

We got our baggage together and were ready to go to a hotel to plan things out when, just as we were leaving the station, Mother began to shout, "Oy, oy, oy, he's here! He's coming!"

"Who's coming, Mother?" I said, confused and a little embarrassed. "The man I told you about, the husband of my cousin, he's coming now."

Before I even had time to wonder how our missing cousin's husband could be here now, Mother had run up to an elegant-looking man and accosted him. He had a small black mustache, and a little pot belly, and was dressed in tasteful black. He bowed to her courteously, and in a moment, she was bringing him over to me.

Up close, he looked even more elegant, as if he had come from a different world. He had just been passing by the bus station in the course of his daily business, he said, and was indeed the husband of Mother's cousin. Right there he invited us to come and stay the night in our cousin's house.

He hired an open carriage for us and our luggage, and drove through the streets of Lublin, then a lovely city of elegant houses. I felt like Natasha in "War and Peace," arriving in St. Petersburg or Moscow for the first time. It seemed a fantasy past fulfillment, yet there I was, wasn't I?

My new cousin's husband's house was elegant, as solid as he was, tastefully arranged, but when we entered, I knew immediately that something was wrong. It was dark and somber inside. An overpowering feeling of sadness pervaded it. Then Tovah, Mother's cousin, came out to greet us.

She looked tired, mournful, and neglected, and there was a lot of unhappiness in her eyes. I just couldn't help staring at her. She took us upstairs to her room, said very little, and left. As we unpacked, Mother told me that they had had a son, an only child, and Mother realized that he must have died recently, which explained her cousin's grieving appearance.

We soon found out that this was indeed the case. The boy had died of pneumonia when he was only six years old, and Tovah had never gotten over it. Where our house in Strzyzow was warm, lively, light, this house was like a cemetery. But I was in Lublin, and if I could, I would stay there, no matter what.

We began discussing it at dinner that night. Tovah's husband, it turned out, was in finance, and very successful. So the cost of putting me up there wasn't an issue. They would gladly take me in, they said, and it wouldn't cost us a penny, even if we offered.

I could hardly believe what was happening. First, the coincidence of meeting him at the station. Now this offer. It was as if God Himself were smiling on me, even in this somber house, as if it were meant to be. I went to bed and woke up in the morning happy in what I knew already was to be my new home.

But first I had to be accepted by a school. The next day we went to a private high school called Czarnecka, which took both Jews and Gentiles. It was an all-girls school with a relatively liberal quota of about 20%, and a reputation for being one of the best in the city. It cost several hundred zlotys a year, a small fortune then. Leah thought about it and talked it over with Tovah and her husband.

"The child really wants it." "It's a good school," I heard them saying. It was a lot of money, but my room and board would be free. I would be far from home, but Tovah and her husband would take good care of me, they promised. And Mother knew they would. They'd really enjoy it, they said, having a child in the house again.

Mother just couldn't say no, so she agreed to do it if I were accepted. I screamed with joy, and when they realized that I had been eavesdropping all the time, we laughed and hugged each other.

The next day Mother and I went to the school and dropped off my transcripts and test scores. A few days later, they told me they would be happy to take me. Soon after, Mother left for Strzyzow; I cried. A whole new life was beginning for me. But I also knew that my old one was ending. What was new was that from the age of 13, I was shaping my own life.

In a short time, I grew close to Tovah and came to call her "Ciotka," (Aunt). In truth she was more like a second mother to me, and I, her missing child. She brought me hot rolls and milk every morning, gave me a nice bedroom, cleaned my clothes and bought me new ones, and made me special things for supper. She didn't give me her son's bedroom, though. That was kept dark and still, with the windows shuttered and the furniture draped. I didn't even like to go near it.

There was little communication between Tovah and her husband, Yankl. He lived in a world different from Tovah's withdrawn sadness. She became my friend, but Yankl remained a stranger. He would look at me in a funny way sometimes. It made me feel uncomfortable. But there was little I could say, nowhere else to go, nothing to do, and no one to talk to about it. I just tried to avoid him and ignore his looks and tentative advances, and just to think about Tovah's constant kindness.

Since the family refused to take money for keeping me, Mother and Father used to send them baskets of food once a week, sometimes twice—farm fresh food, vegetables, fruits, cheeses, jams, breads, and cakes. My Lublin family loved this and looked forward to the packages' arrival, devouring the contents ravenously. I wasn't so excited. It was old hat for me. I had my taste of the farm all my life. What I craved now was the city, that charming sophisticated lovely city of Lublin.

My high school was large, with several red brick buildings on a college-like campus. I studied Latin, French, history, biology, and Polish. I also learned German. Having grown up speaking Yiddish, I picked it up quickly.

In French, I took special tutoring three times a week after school, from two old women with big white caps. I always loved going to their apartment, which smelled of some exotic Indian spice. After the lesson, they would serve me tea and pastries, like in some English movie, I thought.

We all had to wear a special school uniform, a navy blue pleated skirt, a middie blouse with a white sailor collar, and a little hat. The uniform had a number on it, both on the hat and on the collar, and it had to be worn at all times, both in school and out in the street. The school imposed its own curfew on the students, and the number made it easy to distinguish us from any other students in the city, many of whom wore similar uniforms.

It was 9:00 o'clock, which would have been fine in Strzyzow, where there was nothing much to do at night anyway. But I quickly realized it was not quite so acceptable in Lublin.

Just as quickly, I learned that there are ways of the country and ways of the city. The way around this inconvenience was safety pins, little ones. They looked proper during the day at school, but at night, out they came with no number on them, and lots of children in similar uniforms became free. Who would recognize me by my face alone in a big city like Lublin? Nobody.

It was glorious then to be so free. I revelled in the anonymity.

Along with the uniforms at the school came the esthetics, the "morality" of looking natural. No lipstick, no rouge or other coloring. Our hair was to be worn in long braids down the front. But one time I felt adventurous, and had my hair set in a fancy coiffure. On seeing me, the teacher threatened to run water over my head until it washed out. I promised never to do it again.

Yet another time, half on a dare and half on a whim, I went to a beauty shop and got my hair bobbed, almost all cut off.

This time they almost threw me out of the school.

But at home, Tovah bought me nice dresses from some of the best shops in Lublin. I wore heels and stockings for the first time. I was becoming a young city woman, sophisticated and knowledgeable in urban Polish ways, or so I thought. I loved it.

Happily I began to develop many new friendships, a whole new life among girls I was meeting at the school. One girl in particular became a special friend, a Polish girl named Urszula Grande. I am alive today because of her and her family, although the first time we met, we were all a long way from imagining what the future would hold for us.

Urszula's mother was an upper class lady, a little chubby, well spoken and well educated. Her father, tall and energetic, was the Burmistrz, the Mayor of the city. Urszula was beautiful. She had curly blonde hair falling down her shoulders and back in big ringlets. I thought she looked just like Shirley Temple, grown up.

Their apartment was elegant, with polished red-painted wood floors, real Oriental rugs, and in the drawing room, a large grand piano which her mother used to play in the late afternoon and after supper. Urszula and I would stop our talking or reading to sit and listen, drifting off to the music, Chopin, Liszt, Schubert.

Urszula's bedroom was light and airy, all pink and white with a large canopy bed. I would sometimes sleep overnight with her. Looking up, all you could see was the lacy white canopy, like a seamless sky on a clear summer day.

Often in the afternoon, we would go with some of our other girlfriends to one of the coffee shops in the area, for pastries, acting like real young ladies. Or we might buy a kind of hot cake from one of the many street vendors.

I became very close to the whole Grande family, good Polish people who treated me no differently because I was Jewish. I even became friendly with Urszula's older brother, a handsome boy and a star soccer player. They all had thoughts from time to time about making a match between us. I think they wanted to take me into the family, but I knew my own parents would never have consented to it. Marriage to a Christian was one step too far for them, and in truth, for me too. Besides I was too young to be that serious about anybody.

It was not all warmth and beauty and culture in Lublin, however. Not in Poland in the late 1930's. Anti-Semitism is an ancient story in Poland. With Nazi Germany right next door, it had become more unrestrained than ever. I remember one time toward the end of my second or third year in Lublin, I observed an incident in the park near the University. A group of students began to beat up some Jews. They took big sticks and just started to hit the Jews. The University had already tried to establish ghetto benches. This was the beginning of open violence.

I would return to Strzyzow only once or twice a year, once in the winter for a two-week vacation, and then for two months during the summer. When I arrived back at the bus station in Hrubieszow, Father would be there with a carriage to meet me and proudly drive me home, like a father with his yeshiva boy.

Then in my little town I would be treated like a princess. The younger children would bombard me with questions about the latest trends and fashions in the big city, while the older ones would treat me with awe and envy. I sometimes thought it was as if I had come from the moon, the way they looked at me.

But of course I enjoyed the attention and spoiling, and also the simple quiet country times. During those slow sweet summers, I would read and dream, half looking forward to going back to Lublin and my new life, half hoping the summers would last a little bit longer.

The Lublin of 1985 was not the gay and elegant city of my youth, but at least it never suffered the war damage of Warsaw. In the years since I'd last seen it, everything had been allowed to decay little by little, to sag into neglect. Now it was a grey city, drab and depressing. The houses were grey, the public buildings were grey, the police were grey, the people were grey. Everyone seemed sad and cold. I remembered them as being more lively, warmer to each other. Now they walked as if some part of them was missing. The streets were quiet and empty. The stores had nothing in them.

Nevertheless, things about Polish life began to come back to me, things that I had forgotten. Things like kissing a lady's hand. The janitor kisses your hand, the driver kisses your hand, the repairman kisses your hand. I had to smile. It seemed like a gesture out of a comic opera, not something from real life.

In Lublin, one of the first things Jack and I did was to look for my friend, Urszula, and her family. I could not remember the address of their house, so we stopped at the at the Burmistrz's office to inquire. It looked just the same, clean and well-kept, though getting a little shabby. They sent us to the office where official records were kept. There we asked after Pan and Pani Grande. I did not add that they had once saved my life.

The people in the record office could not have been kinder or more helpful, but after hours of searching, they reported that there was no trace of the former mayor or his family. They had a copy of the Grandes' marriage certificate, but nothing after the war. They went through files and files of papers, they made phone calls to other offices and even to Warsaw. They were unbelievably helpful and cooperative, but they could find no information.

It seemed strange that someone as prominent as the Mayor could simply vanish, but when Jack and I talked it over, we remembered that part of Hitler's maniacal assault on Eastern Europe, and especially Poland, had been directed against intellectuals, aristocrats, and political leaders of all kinds, in an attempt to reduce Poles to a leaderless mob. Perhaps a mayor and his family were too prominent. On the other hand, when the Communists took over in Poland, they too "cleaned house."

We left our forwarding address at the records office. The officials said they would keep on checking, and if anything turned up, they would let us know. Just before closing time, we returned with gifts of vodka for the men and perfume for the women, in gratitude for their efforts.

Meanwhile, there was another place in Lublin I had to go see, my old school. When Jack and I turned the corner where I thought it would be, there it was, looking just the same. I started crying, I was so pleased to see it. It was still a school, but state-run of course. I went inside. The school was immaculate, kept up like new. Walking into a class of young girls, I introduced myself to the teacher and spoke to them. I told them I had been a student there too a few years ago. They laughed. The laughter took me back to the good times. I think this was the happiest moment of my whole journey. My life was beautiful when I was in Lublin, so full of hope.

CHAPTER
THREE

The Wait

Toward the end of my third year in high school in 1939, while I was walking on the main street of Lublin, I decided to buy a lottery ticket. They were sold on every street corner for a few zlotys, and I had read in the paper that someone had won a lot of money. Why not? Maybe I'd get lucky too.

And indeed I did. I won 100 zlotys, a lot of money, a few months' tuition. I could have saved it, of course. I'm sure I could have. Or given it to my parents to offset my school expenses, but they didn't want it. They said, "Spend it on something you want. You've worked hard in school. Buy something you want to have, or something you want to do."

Well, they didn't have to tell me twice. There was this trip I knew about, given to my school, a week-long trip to Gdynia, the main port of the Polish corridor to the Baltic, sandwiched between East Prussia to the east, and Germany proper to the west. It was the creation of the Versailles Treaty, and an exciting place to visit. The trip would replace the last week of school, which made it even more attractive. I still loved school, of course, but summer was coming. The air was smelling warm and fresh, even in the morning, and the lure of a new adventure was irresistible.

It was a long trip by train, and when we got there, we were put up in a barracks in Gdynia, nothing fancy, but no matter.

We weren't there for the lodging. Gdynia was full of sailors, young boys, a town bursting with adventures. Of course we weren't supposed to go out at nights, but we found a way to sneak out anyway. We finally did get caught, but not before having enough excitement to last us through the long quiet summer to come.

There were some troubles, though, some bad feelings by the local Germans toward the Poles. Cursing and some street fights. Rocks were thrown. We all got warned to stay away from such things. Someone might get hurt. So during the day, we went to the beaches and to the sailing museums. The week passed all too quickly.

The day before we were ready to leave, we all took a walk by the docks to see the boats and the Baltic before going home. One ship was just casting off, an ocean liner, a grand vision named the *Batory*.

It was full of Hasidic Jews with big bushy beards, and younger boys with the long payess. They were leaving Poland for America that summer of 1939. Something about how they looked just burned into my memory, something so final, so fateful, as if they were taking the last boat out. We all waved to the people on the ship as it left the harbor.

I bought some clothes in Gdynia, before our group returned to Lublin, and then I went back home for the summer. With my new clothes and my stories of my Baltic vacation, I was once again the Queen of Strzyzow. But still, I told Mother, I had a bad feeling about how the Germans acted toward the Poles, as well as the Jews. It just didn't feel good. I was glad to be home this time, safe at home.

My summer was spent reading again, taking books from the library, but also newspapers, full of stories about Hitler, Stalin, the Non-Aggression Pact, the Polish Corridor. It didn't seem so far away any more. I also had time to read *War and Peace* again.

More and more I started thinking about my life and Mother's life. I observed, from a greater distance now, how she lived to help my Father, how Grandmother lived to keep the house, and I knew all this was not for me. I would have to have more, an education at least, perhaps a profession, maybe as a doctor. My life would be different, of that I was certain.

By the summer of 1939, the Polish Corridor, always a point of friction between Germany and Poland, would become yet another of Hitler's testing grounds. Its inhabitants were, by and large, ethnically German. Would they be taken into the Reich like Austria and Czechoslovakia? Or would the world finally stand up to Hitler? Nobody knew.

In March, Hitler demanded a corridor within the corridor, this to run east to west, and to connect Germany and Prussia again. After securing guarantees from England and France, Poland rejected this demand. By August, negotiations between those two countries and Russia for a mutual defense pact had broken down, for, among other reasons, Poland's refusal to grant Soviet troops transit through their country, in case of conflict with Germany. The centuries of hatred, mistrust, and pride held sway.

Later that month, Russia instead signed a non-aggression pact with Germany, containing a secret protocol for the subsequent division of Poland between them. Two days later, on August 25th, Poland signed a formal treaty of alliance with England and France, and mobilization orders went out. Young men were called up immediately, Polish and Jewish alike. Then on September 1, 1939, Germany attacked Poland, and World War II had started.

Despite all the warnings we'd had, we were in shock.

War, actual war, how could it come to this? We all followed the course of the invasion intensely, listening to
radio reports day and night. When the planes passed over-
head, everybody would run down into the cellars to hide.
Most of the fighting, the shelling and bombing, took place
in the large cities like Warsaw and Lublin, but the bom-
bers did not neglect Hrubieszow. We could hear the ex-
plosions from as far away as Strzyzow.

People who had fled from the war areas were strafed by
the Luftwaffe, and many civilians were deliberately gunned
down. We heard horrifying tales from those who had escaped.

Soon, like a second shock, we learned that the Soviet
troops were on their way to occupy Eastern Poland, right up
to the banks of the Bug, in accordance with their secret
protocol. Little Poland was squashed between two mighty
powers, like a swatted fly.

I had already packed my things to go back to Lublin when
the invasion began, but of course my plans were cancelled,
temporarily, we thought. The fighting would be over in a
short while, so we believed. The Polish Army would stop the
Germans and we had Allies to help us now. I remember
thinking how much I was enjoying summer in Strzyzow,
being a celebrity of sorts. I was glad to stay home three more
weeks. Once it was all settled, I'd go back to Lublin and
finish my last year of school, so I could get on with the rest
of my life. For the moment, a few more weeks of vacation
would be nice.

Within a week or two, before September was over, Poland
surrendered to the Nazi Blitzkrieg. By now, England and
France were actively engaged, but for us, the war was over,
and the occupation had begun. Poland soon found itself
divided up into three parts: Wartheland, centered around Poz-

nan in the northwest was incorporated into the 3rd Reich; Generalkommisariat, centered on Bialystok in the northeast was administered by Germans of East Prussia; and the rest, from Warsaw to Przemysl, was something called the Generalgouvernement, which we were a part of. I soon realized I was home for good, for the duration of this horrible war, however long that might be.

In a short time, we began to read about the ghettoes. In Lublin, Warsaw, Lodz, and eventually in Hrubieszow, Jews were herded into dingy, fenced-in slums. Guarded day and night, crowded two and three families to one tiny flat, Jews were allowed out only by special permit, usually to do slave labor for the Germans.

Ghettoes were hardly new for Poland. These were something different from those of the past. People died in them like flies, we heard, sometimes shot down on the street for no reason at all.

In time, we began to see the Russians patrolling on the other side of the Bug. One day, a nice young soldier, tall and dark, in a handsome Cossack tunic, crossed over the river and began to talk to us.

"Come, cross over and go back with us," he said. "It's a brand-new country now, full of opportunity. You can be anything you want in Russia—a doctor, a pilot, a writer. What is there for you here?"

But of course I didn't want to go, to leave everything familiar, and live in a strange country all alone. Still it was tempting, the adventure, the excitement. I wouldn't have to stay forever. "The war will be over soon," I told the soldier. "I must finish high school."

He laughed at me. "It will not be over as soon as you think," he said, "and when the Germans come here to your town, things won't be good for you." I thought back to

Lublin, Gdynia, ghettoes I knew about, and the ones I'd begun to hear about, the refugees shot down on the highways. Finally I went back and spoke to my parents. Lots of people, I said, were going, crossing over the border into Russian-controlled territory. It wasn't hard.

But Mother and Father wouldn't hear of it. Leave everything they'd worked for and built up? Take five children into a strange country with nothing? No, never. "You want to go? You can go. You're young and strong. Maybe it's better if you go. But it's not for us." But I just couldn't go without them. It wasn't that I was too afraid. I just couldn't leave my family.

So we just kept on talking about it among ourselves, and with friends and neighbors. People had different opinions. Everybody in Strzyzow was a politician. We argued about it.

"If we go now," Mother always said, "What would we have? We couldn't take land or a house or a cow." Hard cash, yes, but with eight mouths to feed, how long could that last? If we stayed, we would suffer a little, but the Jews have always suffered, and when the war was over and the wounds were healed, we would at least all still be together in our town, in our own home.

Many others were going. It wasn't that difficult. Some people from Strzyzow crossed over often to visit relatives, and then came home again. My aunt, Mother's sister, went with her husband. They stayed and eventually were swallowed up into Russia in the war. Strangers seeking to cross found many Poles willing to act as guides to the best fording places.

Some of the youngest ones swam across, usually at night, promising to return later to their elders when things settled down. People reasoned that when the Germans came, only the young would be in danger, that the Germans would ignore the helpless older ones. Before the border was closed by the German invasion of Russia, in June of 1941, we could see many refugees from farther west passing through Strzyzow, en route to the Soviet Union. Most came on foot carrying bundles. The lucky ones had hand carts or wheelbarrows for an assortment of household goods. The extremely lucky ones had a horse-drawn wagon.

We owned a horse. Many passing refugees tried to buy it from my Father, but he said no, it was needed in his business. His business? His business was to escape, but of course I only know that now.

By then, we were resigned to a German victory. It might not be so bad, some said. They had more culture than the Poles, certainly, and after the soldiers left, things might get back to normal, maybe better. Maybe under the Germans we'd have less trouble from the Poles, you never know.

So, yes, we sat and waited, as if God had told us to do so, while we watched others from all over Poland passing through and over the border. My family waited, and I waited with them.

Within the year, the Germans had come to our little town, just as that Russian boy had said they would. Armed soldiers were patrolling through it every day, but still no ghetto for the 60 Jewish families.

The soldiers were very careful then during the day, a minority in a strange country showing little violence to Poles or Jews. Outside during the day, they were orderly, disciplined, good German soldiers.

But at night it was different, the bully, the ruffian, the other side, the dark side emerging. They roamed the town freely. This became a horror. They would come into the store, break the windows and the door, throw everything off the shelves, spilling the flour, the sugar, the oil on the floor, drinking and dancing and singing, then leave it all before dawn. Only in the Jewish stores, of course.

When they saw me, I became just another object of their nocturnal excursions. Sometimes they'd break into the house to look for me. My sisters were little girls, so it was only me they were chasing, but we were ready. The house had several exits, and we knew the Germans couldn't cover them all. There were just a few drunken soldiers, nothing organized, so I would sneak out one door and run into the forest where I had played as a child, where I knew I could hide until daybreak. A few times they tried to get me, but they finally gave up.

But still, during the day, they would come by the store, singing a song about Rosalia, the prettiest girl in town. I hid then, too, and prayed with all my might that I would be ugly.

Soon, we began learning about these new Germans. People who had escaped the ghettoes of Warsaw and Lublin told incredible stories as they passed through on their way to the border. They told of people being taken out to be "resettled in the east." They hinted that there were camps that were really secret places for killing Jews.

But nobody believed them. Things were bad enough. There was no need to exaggerate. Still and all, there was something sinister about the Germans. We all knew them better now. Under certain circumstances, it seemed that almost anything was possible.

So we shopped, ate, read. The work in the store went on as before. We began to realize, of course, how bad it was starting to get for others. It was terrible what was happening, but it was happening. Nothing we could do about it now. At least right now it wasn't us, and maybe it will never be us.

Crashing into this heads-in-the-sand world came the news of the invasion of Soviet Russia by Germany. Overnight, the possibility of an easy escape vanished. Just across the Bug, there was no longer a place of refuge—it was now a battleground. Tanks, field guns, armored cars, swarming hordes in uniforms. Every day brought news of new German victories, advancing, advancing, while the surprised Russians fell back in disorder, burning their own countryside behind them.

Soon a battle was raging along a 2400-kilometer front from Leningrad to the Crimea, and by year's end, the Germans were at the outskirts of Moscow. Then suddenly our little Strzyzow was filled with soldiers, most of them wearing on their caps the sinister skull and bones of the SS. Something was about to happen. We didn't know what it was, we didn't dare to imagine.

CHAPTER FOUR

Miaczyn

*Lublin was behind us. We were driving south
toward Strzyzow. Each little village we passed
through reminded me of something—of my trips to
school in Lublin, of my return to Strzyzow after the
German roundups of Jews they called Aktionen, of
many things. But one sign made my heart stop cold—
Miaczin. "Stop!" I said, "Driver, stop here." We
were in a small town like Strzyzow, except that it was
on the railroad. This was the very town, I was sure of
it. But the exact spot, that I couldn't be certain about.*

*"There's an old man. He must have been here in
1941. Ask him." The driver stopped the car, got out,
and approached the elderly passerby. "Some people
in my car," he said, careful not to mention that we
were Jews, "want to see the place where something
happened during the War."*

*"Happened during the war?" The man paused for
thought. "Oh, oh yes, some people were gathered
together and shipped off somewhere. Is that what you
mean?" That was what we meant.*

*"Oh no, not far. A field near the railroad tracks.
Turn that way. . ." We drove there immediately, and
there was the field. Some abandoned box cars were*

lying in it, very like the one I'd ridden in. I started to
cry, and I couldn't stop.

It was a long time really, two and a half years. Yet with
each passing day of those years, we had hoped and believed
it would not come. To others, yes, but not to us. We had done
nothing, but of course that wasn't the point either. What had
the others done? No, it was that we thought we were really
too insignificant, too unimportant, too irrelevant to matter to
the Nazi juggernaut.

And so we thought and waited in that summer of 1942.
Nazi control extended from the Baltic to the Ukraine, and
west to the Atlantic. Leningrad and Moscow still held, and
now the Wehrmacht was massing in the south for the drive
through Stalingrad, the Caucasus, and on into the Middle
East oil fields. Russia, North Africa, Italy. The horrendous
war machine was being extended to the fullest. Labor, soldiers, and supplies were being called up, in insatiably in-
creasing quantities. With all that happening, who could care
about the 60 Jewish families of Strzyzow?

Yet when the call came, no one was really surprised. It
was happening everywhere else with as little reason, as little
logic. So why not to us?

The command came in the middle of the night, from
loudspeakers mounted on trucks that roamed through the
Jewish section of town. The trucks were driven by the so-
called special *milicja*, police, and the order purported to
come from the mayor of Strzyzow. We were to take a few
possessions, just enough for one day, and to assemble in the
town square. We would be picked up by trucks and taken to
the town of Miaczyn ("Myan-chin"), about an hour away.
There we would be "attended to."

So we all packed, Rivka and Ida and I, Dora and David,

and Mother and Father and Grandmother. We all packed and
so did the other 60 families, those who had not crossed the
Bug when it was still possible. We left everything just as it
was in our houses, food in the cold cellar, dishes on the table,
clothes in the closets and trunks, and were routed out door-
to-door by the German soldiers. In a state of numbness and
shock, some of us took odd, inappropriate things for an overnight trip. Candlesticks, bedspreads, big framed pictures. We
assembled in the town square, where huge open-backed
trucks picked us up at dawn, herded in like cattle. We were
taken to a field on the outskirts of Miaczyn. There we
waited. We could see farms in the distance, but no Poles
came to find out what was going on. Railroad tracks ran past
the field, but there was no sign of a train.

We waited with our boxes and our bundles, some clothes,
some jewelry, some food, whatever could be carried easily.
Old and young, children, babies, waiting all day in the sun.
Then all night. Still no train. By then, we were 1,000 or
more, assembled from all the little villages, the tiny
Strzyzows, waiting in an empty field like sheep.

We knew that something very bad was going to happen to
all of us. A labor camp, or worse perhaps. We had heard of
slaughters in the conquered Russian territories, wholesale it
was said. Entire communities shot down and buried in pits.
We couldn't quite believe that though. Labor camp, yes, that
was most likely.

Now too, the doubts came. I should have gone to Russia, I
thought. I was wrong, I should have gone, and now it's too
late. It was a beautiful night in that open field, soft and clear
and full of stars. We could have run away but we didn't.
Where could you run to?

Nobody really believed that Poles would help. We could
still remember the anti-Semitism from before the war, the

"quota," the inscriptions on the walls, and besides, who would risk his family's life to save a Jew?

Some of them helped in exchange for money, or because they were righteous people. But during that night, none of us expected any help from them. We felt that there was no safe place to hide. So who would dare to run away?

But some in fact did run away. Ida, my sweet sister, 14 years old, was one of them. "I don't want to wait," she said, "just to be sent to a camp."

But where would she go? What would she do? She shrugged. She wouldn't say. But when morning came, she was gone, and I've never seen her since.

At dawn, the SS came with their trucks and their dogs. They began to segregate the crowd. There were not many soldiers to manage a crowd of over 1,000. To the left, the younger ones, the able-bodied. To the right, the old ones and the very young. The young ones would work. The old ones and the children? Nobody knew. All you could be certain of was that you did what they said or they would kill you. I saw the Germans shoot a few of us just to make sure we understood that.

I knew where I would go. I turned and looked at my mother. She was what 36, 37? Young and pretty. It was worth a try, I thought. I took off my kerchief and gave it to her. "Put it on and stay with me," I said, "Be my sister, too." Mother smiled, she the mother of five children, but she put it on. She was still holding onto Dora, the youngest girl. Isaac kept David, the little boy. Rivka stayed with me. Ida was gone by then. The two of us older girls passed easily to the left, the side of life. We would make good workers, it seemed. Isaac and David passed through too. Males could also work. They stopped at Mother, looked her over, and wavered for a moment. Still young, yes. She had a small child by the hand. No good. They waved her to the right along with little Dora. And Grandmother, and also our Aunt. The rest of us watched them being marched away to a different fate.

Then the train arrived, and we were hustled into boxcars. Father and the other two into one car, me into another that was all young women, some from Strzyzow and Hrubieszow. My last glance of Mother, she was holding my little sister Dora, and still wearing my kerchief. At that time I'd never heard of the Sobibor Death Camp.

> *I know Mother and Grandmother and Dora are gone, ashes now. I know where Father and David and Rivka are buried. It's Ida I think about.*
>
> *If she is still alive, she would be in her early 60's. Did she reach Russia? No, surely not. By then, it was hundreds of kilometers away. Did she find a compassionate Polish family to take her in? She was smart. She would know what to do. If only fate granted her a tiny piece of luck, it's possible she could have survived like me.*
>
> *But if so, she must have passed for a Pole. Would she give up her disguise now, if say by some miracle she was located? I don't know, I just don't know, but I've never given up hope.*

CHAPTER
FIVE

Chelm

After the Aktion, the mass seizure of Jews in Miaczyn in 1942, I was transported by boxcar to the vicinity of Chelm, about halfway between Hrubieszow and Lublin, the same Chelm immortalized by Sholem Aleichem in his tales of the "Naronem" (Fools). From there, we girls were taken to a nearby farm and relieved of our few possessions. I worried about where they had taken Father and David and Rivka, hoping we would be reunited. It was this hope and faith that kept me believing, and gave me the strength to go on.

We all settled in for the night, sleeping wherever we could. It was summer and still quite warm in the evenings. I found a nice clean hayloft above a barn.

It was a Polish farm with Polish families still living on it, and in the surrounding neighborhood. They ran the farm under the supervision of a few German guards. Not many were needed to supervise mere women, they must have felt. So I didn't have to work too hard, and there wasn't that much I knew anyway. What did I know about cows, chickens, and farming? What I knew was from books, from the store, and from Lublin. Besides, I had other things on my mind, like escape. It looked so easy. The few guards we had couldn't be everywhere. They counted on the fact that Jews in a strange and hostile Polish countryside would have nowhere to go and would not think of escaping. But, I thought, I might be able to pass as a Pole once I got away from the farm. It had happened often enough in Lublin. It was dangerous, but so was being there. I decided I would try it. Just waiting around wasn't for me.

But first, I had to get some new clothes. I thought and watched for a few days, and finally asked one of the Polish girls who lived on the farm to help me. She looked like a fair person, a good person, though you could never know for sure.

"I have to leave," I said to her, "to search for my family. Will you help me?" The girl told me she had no great love for the Germans, and gave me one of her dresses.

I waited a few more days just to be sure. Then after about a week on the farm, I got up one morning, put on my clean new dress, and walked out. Nobody paid much attention. Nobody stopped me. I don't know what I would have done if they had. I had never thought about it.

Once outside, I felt almost safe. I spoke Polish like a Pole, better than most I always thought. On the road walking away from the farm, I just tried to look and act like any other Polish girl on her way to the city. I carried a basket on my arm as if I were going to town to sell something. There was nothing in the basket, but nobody stopped me to look.

Later in the day, someone did stop to offer me a ride to town in a car. There weren't many civilian cars on the road in those wartime days. I politely declined because I didn't want to make any more conversation than I had to.

It was only after I was some distance from the farm toward the end of the day that I noticed a few zlotys stuck in the pockets of my dress. I stopped and stared at them. The money was a gift from the girl at the farm and I didn't even know her name. Feeling strange, I kept walking.

By nightfall, I reached Chelm and found my way to the

Jewish ghetto. I immediately started asking for people I knew, and soon located a cousin of my Father's. He was amazed to see me, more so when he heard how I had "escaped." They had a good laugh at the Germans, the vaunted "master race," the "ubermenschen," who couldn't even keep a young girl for a week. After washing and a meal, we went together to ask around about my family. Others had run away too, from other farms or camps or transports, and they might know who was heading where and what had happened to my family. We put the word out.

Nobody there seemed to know about Mother and Dora. No one who had seen them had made it back to the ghetto. As for Ida, she had vanished that night, but someone had seen Father and David and Rivka, alive on a work farm right near Chelm. I decided I would go to the farm and see if I could find them. It was a big risk, and they all tried to discourage me. I should at least wait, they said, to see if they too might escape on their own. But I was adamant. I knew where they were. They were the only family I did know about for certain. I was going to try to get them out.

I guess I was young, innocent, naive. At 19, you don't believe anything bad can really happen to you. A few years later, would I have felt the same way, done the same thing? I don't know.

One argument I had made was that there was a precedent in our family for such a thing. During the First World War, toward the end, my aunt's brother was arrested by the Czarist police for being a radical. My aunt, afraid for his life, left her family, her husband, and her three small children, and walked all the way from Lublin to Hrubieszow to plead for him. She went directly to the Russian Chief of Police and begged for his release, which indeed followed shortly after. So, I argued, a certain amount of boldness, of bravado, might impress the authorities. I'd never know until I tried. Anyway, when they saw I was going to do it, no matter what they said, Father's cousins gave me some new clothes, some money and their blessing. "It's crazy, but if she's going, she's going," they grumbled. Who really knew any more what made sense?

The work camp near Chelm was a self-contained village, mostly Jews with a few Poles, set by the edge of a small stream, a tiny tributary of the Bug. It contained about 800 workers in torn and dirty clothes, with yellow star armbands and the word, "Juden" stencilled on their front and back. Their job was to dig around the edge of the river bank, setting pilings in the soft earth. No one was sure why, though the consensus was that the Germans had ordered the project because it was such hard work that it would kill most of the Jews soon enough, and those who didn't die right away would be too tired to escape. They figured that when they were finished there, if any of us were still alive, they would just have to move on and start all over again some place else.

There were no fences, but lots of guards and dogs. Very few Jews actually did try to escape, and fewer still succeeded. There was no place to go, and for the men, it was more difficult to hide as Poles. If someone suspected a man, all they had to do was to pull his pants down to check his penis, and he was finished.

There was no real camp headquarters, since this was still physically a village, so when I got there, I asked one of the soldiers where the Commandant was. The soldier looked at me, saw a well-dressed, well-spoken young Polish woman, and offered to take me there himself. I said that wouldn't be necessary, just point out the house. He shrugged and did so. I made my way over to the house he had pointed to, an appropriated farm house, not so different from my own back in

Strzyzow. When I asked to see the Commandant, I was shown in. He was in his early 30's, and nice enough looking for a German soldier. His air was one of complacent boredom, as if he already knew that nothing very exciting or challenging was likely to happen to him for the rest of this war. "Yes, what do you want?" he asked me in German. I nodded and asked if I could speak to him in Polish. He waved his hand, "Get on with it."

"Please, I came here about my father and brother and sister," I began. "They're here, and they're very sick." I stopped to look for the smallest trace of sympathy or understanding in his eyes. All I saw was astonishment, but I had to go on.

In fact, I didn't really know if Father and the others were dead or alive, sick or well, or even that they were actually there. But I believed they were and wanted to make the best case possible. The Commandant certainly wouldn't know one way or the other.

"They're all I have left in the world," I went on. "The rest of my family is gone. If only I could take them out of here, back to the ghetto in Hrubieszow." From flabbergasted, the expression on his face was turning, I thought, into faint amusement that a Jewish girl would have the nerve to walk in here just like anybody else, with no papers and no protection, and ask for something so outrageous. I'm sure nothing so outrageous had happened to him since he had been assigned to this dreary backwater camp. I certainly hoped so— it wasn't something that would work too often.

We talked a little more, and I sensed his growing admiration for my improbable boldness. At least, I prayed that's what he was feeling. After a while, he signalled a soldier just outside the open door. In German, he told the soldier to take me to the people I asked for, and then to escort me back to his office. He emphasized "escort" deliberately, in a very proper and formal fashion.

I of course understood what he was saying, and couldn't stop myself from smiling, despite my pretension not to know German. He saw the smile and shook his head. I was full of surprises.

Bowing slightly, I thanked him in German. He waved me out, then sat watching me through the window as I walked down to the river bank with the soldier.

There was Father with the others, digging holes in the moist earth, looking pale, drawn, half-dead. My brother David sat nearby. He could no longer walk. Rivka was not in sight.

Father was frightened when he saw me. "What are you doing here, my child. What will they do to you?" Clearly I was not a prisoner. Then what else could I be?

"Poppa, I'm going to get you out of here," I said. "I don't know how, but I will." I looked around. "Rivka?"

"She's here," Isaac answered. He shrugged. "Not well, but with us here. Your Mother?" he went on, the weight of the question mark heavy upon him. "No news yet," I said. "Still checking, still hoping."

We talked a while as I told them about my meeting with the Commandant. I could have been killed for trying it, but here I was.

While we talked, the German soldier who had escorted me there, sat down and watched the river. Better than the Russian front, especially on such a soft summer day. When we finished, he led me back to the Commandant. I went in and closed the door behind me. We talked briefly. Then I walked alone out of the camp, back to the town and the ghetto.

The next day I came back to the camp, but this time in a rented closed carriage. A carriage, a driver, and me, Rosalia

Orenstein, driving right into the camp and up to the Commandant's office. I stopped there, spoke briefly to him, and got a pass for Father and David and Rivka to leave the camp.

Then I went down with a soldier to get them. Isaac and David were together. Rivka was sent for. They all looked weak and frightened. "Poppa, I'm going to take you out of here now," I said to him. He still couldn't really understand or believe it.

"But how can you do that, my child. Look how we look, how we are dressed." I smiled, led them all up the hill a bit, and proudly showed them the carriage. If it had been a space ship, it could not have seemed more outlandish to them.

The driver nodded to the covered area just behind the back seat. He remained perched high on his own seat, holding the horse's reins, while the three of them, Father, David, and Rivka, got in and hid themselves behind the back seat. I sat in the front seat which faced backwards, down toward them. The driver whipped the horse, and we drove out of the camp and through the entire village, past groups of workers who saw only a young Polish girl out for a drive in a carriage. I smiled sweetly at some of them as we passed by.

The carriage took us to Chelm, where we all got out. But I wasn't quite finished yet. I had promised my cousin, Zailyk Herbst, in Chelm that I'd try to get his father out too. There in the camp, I had seen his father. The next day I did go back, this time carrying something extra with me, a little present for the Commandant.

Cousin Zailyk had a few things of value left, silver from melted down candlesticks and tableware, about two kilos altogether. When I got in to see the Commandant this time, I lay it out in front of him and he took it, still with that faintly amused look on his face. In truth, it wasn't really worth that much money, but it was the principle of the thing, I think.

Fortunately, Gary's father was released to me, and I took him back in the same carriage to Chelm. Gary couldn't say enough to thank me. We began a celebration that lasted all night, a celebration dampened only by the thought of those who were not there, of Leah, of Dora, and Ida, of Grandmother, of all the others who were still missing.

A few days later, my family made our way on foot back to Hrubieszow, and the relative safety of the ghetto there. Later on during the war, I heard that the Commandant who had helped me had been denounced by someone, and taken away by the Gestapo. I was sorry when I heard about it.

We all waited for several weeks in the Hrubieszow ghetto. I tended to those who were weak or sick, as we all waited for word of Leah and the others to filter back, but none ever did. Word of other ghettoes, bigger ghettoes, did come through, but now instead of overcrowding, we began to hear of them being emptied out in those periodic German "procedures" called *"Aktionen."* The Jews had been taken off somewhere to camps, it was said, and never heard of again. This was still hard to believe, but was accepted as true as time went on.

It might not be such a good idea to wait around too much longer, I began to tell myself. Father, who, because of the store, was a middleman for many Polish farmers in the area, thought we could all hide out on one of those farms. He knew a man named Jedgycz, a good Polish man, and Father was sure he would hide us all until the war was over.

At the beginning, I thought this would be a good idea. I felt relieved. We would stay together, and then we would try to find Dora, Mother, and Grandmother. But it was Father who decided that I should leave them, and try to survive. He was trying to persuade me that my chances of staying alive would be greater then. I didn't look Jewish at all. I spoke perfect Polish, and I was energetic and intelligent, so I could easily pass as a Pole without being discovered, or even suspected.

"With that lovely hair and those eyes of yours," he said, "nobody will ever think you are not a Pole."

I tried to argue with Father, saying that now, while Dora, Mother, and my youngest sister, Ida, were no longer with us, they were all I had. I didn't even want to listen to the idea of leaving them, I loved them so much, but my Father kept urging that I should try to survive for their sake, for him, for Rivka, and David, and when everything was over, I would come back and together we'd find Dora and Mother.

"You know enough about the Catholic religion," he said, "You had so many Polish friends. It will be easier for you and for us. You must go, and may God be with you there. We must separate to survive."

I listened to his words with my heart breaking into pieces, and cried. What arguments could I present? Deep in my heart, I knew he was right. We had to separate to save our lives. I was 19 and a woman, and I had to try whatever kind of luck I could find, but I wanted to postpone the farewell moment. Already I had seen and heard of too many cruelties and deaths. I strongly believed that nothing bad could happen to my family, but when it came time to say goodbye, I looked at them with tears running down my cheeks, and that sinking feeling in my heart, "Will I ever see them again?"

And so we parted. Father, David and Rivka set out for the nearby farm, leaving at night and arriving before dawn, and I left the same day to follow my own path which would at first take me down the road I had traveled before, this time not headed to Strzyzow but back to Lublin. That road always before had led to my future, but where it would take me now, I did not know.

CHAPTER SIX

Polish Girl

Before I started down the road alone in that summer of 1942, I took off my Star of David and my yellow star and became a Polish girl once again. I was on my way to Lublin, which had been so much a part of my old life, the place where I had grown from a girl to a young woman. No particular plan was in my mind. I just couldn't think of any other place to go.

Making my way toward Lublin, I walked for the most part, but now and then, when I asked for a ride from farmers or tradesmen passing down the road in their horse-drawn carts, I tried not to make too much conversation. When pressed, I told them my parents belonged to the Polish partisans and were in hiding now, that I was going to Lublin to stay with friends until my parents could come and get me. In those days it was not an unusual tale, and it raised little comment.

On the second day in mid-morning, while passing a fruit orchard near Miaczyn, a city in which my family and I had been rounded up only a few weeks ago, I saw a group of Nazi soldiers in the distance, not ordinary soldiers but an SS killing squad, an Einsatz Gruppe. From where I was, I could only see their telltale dark cuffs and sleeve insignia. They were the shock troops of the "Final Solution," assigned to carry out mass murders right out in the fields.

I heard, as I approached on trembling legs, the unmistakable sounds of guns. A few more minutes and I would be upon them. The freshly dug trenches, the mass graves of an extermination site being filled with still warm naked bodies, the cries and moans of those still alive all would be before me. By now I had heard these stories often enough.

Still, I couldn't believe it. This was like a movie. I was watching a nightmare, I was dreaming. Why wasn't I waking up? And here it was, only a few hundred yards ahead.

My head swam, my stomach heaved, I was weak with terror and disgust. What kind of Polish girl would be walking alone now on this road? If I kept on, I would walk right into the thing, become part of it. I dropped to my knees and crawled over to the sloping shoulder of the road, down toward the weeds edging the adjacent orchards.

The sound of their voices and laughter echoed in my direction as they finished their job. A few last stray shots, and they were off again, marching toward me down the road. I closed my eyes, thinking, just thinking and wondering which side of my head they would hit me on when they reached me. Left or right, front or back? The fear, the heat, the tension made me so tired, so weak that I kept my eyes closed, still listening to the footsteps and joking banter, and waiting for the crushing impact of the blow to come. And it came, but softly, as in a dream. Soft as a mother's caress, which in the dream it was. Mother, caressing my head, telling me to lie still there, my child, and rest, and everything will be all right.

Then in a moment, Mother told me to sit up and to eat some of the apples she was holding out for me, nice juicy red apples. The air was quiet, the road empty. "Eat these apples, my Raisele, eat them and then leave here. It's not safe for you. Go away from here. Eat the apples, my child, and leave."

When I awoke, I found myself lying there by the edge of the road, only half-hidden by the weeds, my legs still sticking out, the soldiers gone. Perhaps they had not seen me, perhaps they imagined me dead already; I dared not look to find out.

> *Mother, for a second time you gave me life, for I'm certain you did come to me there beside a Polish road, and tell me to lie quiet until danger was past, and then tell me rouse up to move on. I know about Sobibor by now. Somebody told me much later that you and Dora and Grandmother and Auntie were there on your way to death, but that wasn't the end for you. You came back to give me life again.*
>
> *I'm on my way back to Strzyzow now to look for Father and Rivka and little David. I'll give them your love.*

I arose and wandered into the orchard, coming finally to a Polish farmhouse. There I knocked on the door and was invited in. I told the story of my parents in the Partisans in my best Polish, and they took me in for a few days, cleaned me up, fed me, and gave me some new clothes and money so that I could take the bus the rest of the way to Lublin. They told me to be careful. It was not safe for a young girl alone in this country any more.

Not knowing or caring whether they believed my story, I thanked them and left. Now I knew I was truly on my own. I would have to be smart, smarter. I'd been lucky so far. God, a dream, Mother, something had protected me. But from now on, my life would be in my own hands, to hold onto or to lose.

It was the same kind of bus as when I first came to Lublin to find a high school, arriving at the same station where I'd first met Mother's cousin, but now there were no Jews to be seen at the station or on the streets. And that sad and somber house that had been my home for three years was deserted and forlorn, because now the Jews of Lublin were gone, taken away by those transport trains, the ones that left full "to the eastern territories for resettlement," and came back empty.

And yet the city looked almost the same, all but untouched by the war. The war was in Russia or Africa, thousands of miles away, not here in the heart of Nazi-held Europe, but I no longer felt like a part of it. I no longer felt like a part of anything.

There was still one place I could go, one family that still might take me in. Urszula's family, Urszula Grande, my high school friend, and her father, the Burmistrz, the Mayor. They had always wanted to fix me up with Urszula's older brother, to make me one of the family. Maybe now they would take me in to save my life.

Finding the Grande apartment house was no trouble. I walked as if I knew just where I was going, and as if I belonged there. A Polish girl, a little down on her luck, not at all unusual in those days in Lublin, ordinary, unexceptional. When I knocked on the front door, a maid answered, a new one. From behind her, I heard the afternoon sounds of the piano, dreamlike in their familiarity. Chopin, Liszt, civilized sounds. I asked for Mrs. Grande, and waited as the maid went to get her.

"Moj Baze!" she said as she opened the door. "My God, is it you, Rosalia, I don't believe it." She made the sign of the

Cross as if to attest to the miracle of seeing me on her doorstep. I stood there nodding, "Yes, it's me. Yes, it's me. Yes, it's me."

"Come in, come in!" she said, after what seemed to me, knowing the dangers, to be a very long time standing outside. "Come in and tell me what has happened to you." Then she turned and called for Urszula to come and see who was here.

I told them my story quickly and simply. I'd thought about it so much, gone over it in my mind so often.

"I'm alone now, on my own," I ended up, and they said that of course they would take me in. They didn't say for how long, and I didn't ask.

After I got washed up, they gave me Urszula's bedroom, the pink and white room with the single bed covered by a pink canopy, the two little Oriental rugs on the polished hardwood floor, and the white furniture. It was like something out of a Hollywood movie, a room that felt like all the safe and warm and clean things in the world, wrapped up in one pink and white package. They didn't ask me any more questions right then, and Urszula came and gave me a big hug that made me cry.

Then they fixed a big dinner for me of flacki, a sweet and sour dish made of stewed pieces of a cow's stomach, wrapped in intestines. Not kosher, of course, but I would have eaten sand then, I was so hungry.

We didn't talk much at dinner, and Mr. Grande signalled that whenever the servant was in earshot, no mention was to be made of my recent history or background. In these times, you could trust no one. After dinner, Urszula's mother went into the living room to play the piano as always, sweetly, almost timidly just as before, and after a while, I started to cry, trying to hide it as the thoughts of the dead and the missing, of my danger and hunger and homelessness flooded my mind. Right here before me, people could play the piano, and live in a nice clean warm house as if nothing had changed since I had come there as a child.

When she stopped playing and the room was quiet, she looked at me and could see that it was time for me to get some sleep. "Rougea," she said, calling me by my childhood name, "Rougea, lie down now, you're tired." And she took me up to Urszula's room.

The next morning we all had breakfast together like one big family, like the old days as schoolmates. Urszula's father went off to work, and Urszula and I helped her mother around the house a little, then sat and talked about all that had happened to us in the three years we had been apart.

When her father came back from work, however, he said it was time for a serious discussion. We all went into the living room and waited for him to begin.

The whole family, he started, was in great danger with me there. If the Nazis should find out, they would not only kill me, they would kill the entire family. Hiding a Jew was a capital crime. It was not fair to put them all in such danger.

"Furthermore, since I am the Mayor," he went on, "and in the public eye, it's only a matter of a short time before Rose is discovered here. We have to act quickly."

"Why not," suggested Mrs. Grande, "send her to friends or relatives in a different city where she could hide for the rest of the war?"

But the Burmistrz shook his head. "Poland is a small country. If she is ever discovered anywhere, it will be very easy to trace her back to us. Besides if she arrives in some small town alone with no family, no friends, no visitors, just by herself, she will raise suspicions, and once they start checking, we will all be in great danger.

All this was true. I couldn't deny it. He went on. "I have another idea. I've been thinking about it all day at work. The child should go to Germany."

"Germany! But how, why?" Mrs. Grande was aghast. "A Jew in Germany is a dead Jew. This girl is like a daughter to me." She cried. I said nothing, I was numb. Whatever they wanted to do was all right with me. They had already done so much.

"Be calm, my dear," he said, very much the Mayor. "I've thought this out carefully. In my office, I have many sets of papers, identification papers for Polish girls, Christian girls who have died or vanished in Lublin. Girls who would be your age." Then I understood. I would go to Germany disguised as a Polish girl once again. He turned to me.

"But you will have to go by yourself to register for work in Germany. I can give you identification papers, but I cannot risk being seen with you in case there is a problem."

Whatever you must do, you should do, I reminded myself, watching his face closely, and once I got over the first shock, this idea, however strange, made sense to me. Lots of people were going to Germany now. The German workers were in the army, and there was a great demand for foreign labor. I had read about it many times.

The wages were low, but better than what you could get in war-torn Poland. For some, it was a kind of adventure. For most, it was a way to survive. And certainly, who would think to look for a Jewish girl there, hiding in the very belly of the beast. It was risky, but if it worked, both the family and I would be safe for awhile.

"All right," I agreed, "what must I do?" And so it was decided. The papers were prepared. I would no longer be Rosalia Orenstein, a Jewish girl from Strzyzow. I was now

Kazimiera Lukashuk, a displaced Polish girl from Wlodimierz, Poland.

Urszula and I practiced my story together to go along
with the papers. We made it as simple as possible. I'd had
a fight with my parents and was looking for a better life in
Germany. I got myself ready to go and make my applica-
tion. Putting on my dress that Marysia's aunt had given
me for my walk to Lublin, not new, not too clean but
decent looking, I asked Mrs. Grande what she thought.
She said the dress was too good looking for the story I
would be telling.

She took care of it that night, making a dress for me out of
some leftover fabric she had around, heavy rug fabric, the
sort of thing a poor girl in a desperate situation might have to
wear. While she sewed, I rehearsed my speech. When I finally finished, we all went to sleep.

The next morning, wearing that dress, I walked into the
Immigration Office, an official German office for recruiting
foreign labor into the Reich. I was greeted perfunctorily by a
stern-looking woman in steel-rimmed glasses who told me to
sit down and wait. She was typing and continued on for a
few minutes longer before turning back to me.

"Why do you want to go?" she asked with no great interest. I was ready. "I've had enough here," I said calmly in my
almost too-perfect Polish. "Things are not so good for me. I
heard Germany is beautiful. I have no money. I'm not going
to school. I've got no reason to stay. My parents are far
away. I had a fight with them anyway—we don't get along.
And I want to see a little of the world. Maybe in Germany I
can make something of myself."

The woman in steel-rimmed glasses listened. She had
heard this story 1,000 times already, 50 times that day. She
told me to come back in two days to take the transport train

to Germany. She didn't say where in Germany, and I didn't ask.

At Urszula's apartment, they were overjoyed to hear that the plan had worked. Now they hoped that all of us might be safe. But still, the night before I was to leave, their home was filled with tears. We knew we would never see each other again, despite all the promises we were making of the wonderful reunion we would have when it was all over. Life in those days overflowed with unkept promises.

> *We never did meet again. After the war, I was still in hiding, and later on, I left Poland for America. Only now have I been able to come back and look. No luck. Where is Urszula? Is she still alive? I don't know. But I have one sad thought, that she is alive but would no longer admit to knowing me, to having helped me. In Poland, it is still not so popular to help the Jews.*
>
> *But maybe not. Maybe one day I will find her, and we will hug each other and tell each other about our lives, just as we did then back in her gauzy-white bedroom in Lublin. I am still hoping.*

CHAPTER SEVEN

Germany

Getting ready to go to the station, I put on my just-made "old dress," so I would look the part I now had to play, but underneath I wore my good Lublin dress. There was some food in a bag, a change of underwear, and a few zlotys Mr. Grande had insisted I take, and that was about it.

Mr. Grande had not let his wife or daughter accompany me to the station—too risky. So we all kissed and hugged and said our tearful goodbyes on the steps of their apartment in an area made private by a wall. As I left, I closed the door on that chapter of my life forever.

The station was crowded with many young men and women, looking much like myself. Thank God for that, I thought, especially as I watched the patrolling SS men with submachine guns and dogs straining on their leashes, magnificent German shepherds, trained to sniff out Jews, I figured. I clutched my package of bread and cheese to my breast, hoping the dogs wouldn't take an interest in it, but I made it onto the train with no problems, and once on board, I felt safer, if not completely safe.

We were headed for Koln (Cologne), or more precisely, Leverkusen, the huge industrial complex on the Rhine, manufacturing site of chemicals and medicines for decades, since the days of the Kaiser. Aspirin had been invented there in the 1890's.

But now they made other kinds of chemicals, using other kinds of workers. Their normal work force had been depleted by the war, and young semi-skilled trainable labor was desperately and constantly needed.

Thus this transport train was comfortable and inviting, a normal coach with plush seats, immaculately clean, and unobtrusively patrolled. We were not prisoners, we were recruits going to work for the greater good of the Third Reich. The journey lasted more than two days and nights, across almost the entire width of both Poland and Germany, over 1,500 kilometers. I watched the scenery, watched my traveling companions, ate my food until it was gone, and when night fell, lay back to sleep, but could not. Every 10 minutes, a soldier walked down the central corridor, checking on the slumbering passengers. Wearing my secret of a double life like the two layers of clothing on my body, I felt this was hardly the time to relax. I couldn't and didn't, and instead, watched the moon outside the compartment window, and listened to the breathing of those who would, from now on, be sharing my fate.

Late that night, as I was thinking why I couldn't and shouldn't relax, I drifted off into an awkward sleep sitting in my seat. Suddenly I awoke to hear a girl's voice speaking Yiddish, talking and mumbling about her mother and her brothers in a camp, as if my own deepest terrors had surfaced and become vocal. For one terrifying instant, I thought it was me, but no, I wouldn't have spoken in Yiddish. I understood it from hearing my Grandmother at home, but I always spoke to her in Polish. Polish was my primary language, the language of my dreams

So if these weren't my dreams, whose were they? As the

first frightful vision passed, and as I got hold of myself, I heard the voice again. "Mammala. . . kayna horeh," repeating the story of a fight and a camp, all in Yiddish.

Now I was fully awake. My own fears of discovery transferred to this unknown girl, this other secret Jew. I heard the sounds of the approaching SS men. I could see the girl now, only a few seats away from me, still mumbling in her sleep. The SS were getting closer.

With sudden resolve, I leaned out and gave her a slap on the face as fast as I could. The girl gave one last gasp in Yiddish, "Oy, Mammala." Then came the stunned realization of what she had said. She froze, eyes staring open. Where was she? Who had heard? The SS?

The footsteps of the guards grew louder. The young girl glanced around quickly. Everyone else seemed to be sleeping. Maybe she had dreamed the slap too. The soldier came up to her seat and walked past without missing a beat. She was not discovered.

I watched her carefully for a while after that. She didn't go back to sleep. She obviously did not know who had awakened her. Indeed, she probably thought the slap was part of her dream.

And I was not about to tell her otherwise yet. Even to know her secret was dangerous, but for her to know mine could be fatal, especially because she was the one who was talking in her sleep.

When we arrived at Koln-Leverkusen, we were divided in sections, each going to a different part of the factory complex. I was grouped with my secret companion, strictly by chance. We even ended up in the same barracks, but still not a word was said between us. As the transport was unloaded, we saw that a number of Poles were there, watching. Some must have been looking for friends and family to join them.

Others probably were searching for a familiar face among the laborers. Still others were just curious.

Among them was a tall young man, quite handsome, keen-eyed, who seemed to have a special interest in me. I did my best to avoid him. I did not want him to have a close look at me. Does he remember me from somewhere, I wondered? My heart pounded. Strzyzow? I would recognize him. Hrubieszow? Possibly. Lublin? More likely. Some place where I was known as Rosalia, known as a Jew.

But we all went on to our barracks, transported there by buses, and nothing more was said or done. The barracks were newly made wooden structures with 10 rows of beds on each side of a narrow aisle, three tiers of beds in each row. Not even as nice as the hayloft at the work camp, but at least the place was clean.

As soon as we got settled in, washed up a bit, and changed our clothes, a German soldier came in and called out the name, "Kazimiera Lukashuk." I went about my business, unpacking and settling in while the soldier waited and then called out the name again, "Kazimiera Lukashuk." My God, I suddenly realized, that's me. I ran up to the soldier, so concerned about my lapse of attention that I didn't have time to worry what this was about. The soldier told me that someone wanted to see me.

Then the fear came over me. Discovered already? Maybe someone else heard the Jewish girl talking in her sleep, or saw me wake her. Maybe someone, that tall Pole, perhaps, recognized me. I was led into a little anteroom off my barracks, and there he was, the tall Pole who had been staring at me at the station. Whatever this was all about, I had to brazen it out. He waited until the German soldier had left us alone, and then leaned over and whispered to me softly, so as not to be overheard.

"Don't worry," he said in Polish, "I'm a friend. I saw you at the station and got your name from the transport records. You looked like a bright girl, and I wanted to help you. If you ever need anything, have any trouble, want more food perhaps, you just ask for me." He stopped for a moment, and I just nodded. "My name is Wladek," he went on. "Now tell me, what brought an intelligent girl like you to this place?"

A feeling of relief flooded over me, warming me like a hot bath. So he doesn't know anything after all. He wants to be a friend. Fine. Less tense, I smiled at him. If he doesn't know anything and I don't tell him anything, he can't hurt me. That's a good friend these days, the best you can expect.

So I told him a variation of the story I told the lady with the steel-rimmed glasses, about my parents in Wlodimierz, and the fight and wanting to see some of the world and make something of myself, and he seemed to believe me. Before we parted, he told me again that he was going to look out for me. He smiled a nice smile when he said it. A clever smile, and I believed him, thinking that maybe he too knew more than he was saying. Everyone had something to hide in those days.

In the morning, I was assigned to a job in a nearby laboratory. I was taught to take specific gravity measurements of samples of newly developed plastic materials, by weighing them both before and after immersion in a water bath.

It was exacting, tedious work, but I proved to be quite adept at it. It was a good job, quiet, clean, with little physical strain. The pay was minimal but it did include both housing and food. The lab itself was clean and bright and white, with large windows in bauhaus style. I even wore a white coat when I was working, like a doctor. There were, I thought, a lot worse ways to spend the war.

After a few weeks, the supervisor of my lab began to come over to my table, acting very friendly. He was a little older than I, almost 30, to me practically ancient, a German of course, though he spoke decent Polish to all his Polish workers. He spoke German to the others, which I understood too, although I never let on about this. The less you seemed to understand, the safer you might be. This supervisor, it seemed, had more on his mind than just efficient work. He knew that the food rations for the foreign laborers like me were only barely sufficient nutritionally, adequate for light work perhaps, but not exactly exciting. So every day or so, he would come over and slip half a sandwich, maybe a whole one, ham or knockwurst or chicken, into my desk with a small smile. "A present," he would say, though maybe not really a free gift, that smile implied.

I always took the sandwich—I didn't want to get him angry. But I always left it there in my drawer without touching it. No matter how hungry I was, I never ate it. I didn't offend him by refusing it. This after all was a good job, and I didn't want to lose it. But I couldn't take gifts from a German, not food, not anything. I waited until he left the lab. Then I buried the sandwich in the refuse underneath the trash bin, or took it out of the lab in my purse and threw it away later. Yes I was hungry often, and they were good sandwiches, but I wasn't going to take anything from him, not from a German.

My barracks was made up primarily of Polish girls, with a few from other countries of the occupied "Greater Reich." Czechoslovakia, Romania, Latvia, Estonia. They had come from all over to this city of factories, Leverkusen, to work for Bayer and Agfa-Gevaert, making aspirin and film and industrial chemicals, Plexiglas and plastics. That tall Polish boy, Wladek, who had first noticed me in the train station, now came to visit me often in the barracks, sometimes every other day, to take me out for a walk and often to give me some extra food.

I gladly took it from him, amusing him with my habit of gobbling everything down immediately in one sitting. I did this even with my normal evening rations in the barracks, the soup and bread and margarine, given only three times a week. I always ate it all at once, even if I might go hungry the next day. If you stretched it out, you were always hungry anyhow. This way, at least for a few hours, you were satisfied.

Wladek always treated me with respect and never made any sexual advances, though we both I think were considering it. But you had to be careful. One of the Polish girls in my barracks had gotten pregnant by another Polish worker. She was so young and now her life was so complicated. The boy, Stanislav, they called him Lada, was very sweet, but he was in no position to take care of her, much less with a baby. I felt so sorry for both of them.

So, I was very careful with Wladek, very cool and reserved in every way. I listened very closely to him when he talked. He seemed to know the ins and outs of everything, whom you had to know and what you had to do to get anything done, and he had fascinating stories to tell. About the Polish Resistance, and the Partisans fighting behind the German lines.

I didn't know how he knew all that, and didn't ask, but I was getting a feeling that he too was hiding something. Maybe he also sensed that in me, and that's why we were drawn together. But we both knew enough not to ask too much. It was best for many reasons to keep that respectful safe distance.

In every way I could think of, I tried to be careful, I tried to be smart. Yet I was a young woman then, hardly more than a girl, and sometimes you make mistakes, even if you follow the most natural and obvious choices. So finally, I did confide in someone, someone I thought surely I would be safe with.

It was the young Jewish girl whose life I had saved on the train coming there, living in the same barracks, eating together, talking together at night, doing the laundry. Naturally we got to know each other.

Her Polish name was Helena, the name she always went by in the barracks. She did look Jewish, more so than I did. Some of the other girls commented on it to me. "Look at her. She looks like a Jewess, doesn't she," and I told them they were crazy, but it worried me.

Yet, I was alone, living my secret life, knowing Helena's secret while she did not know mine. One day while we were doing laundry together with no one else around, I just happened to tell her, "Listen, I know who you are."

"What do you mean?" Her face grew blank, hard, a mirror of the way my face looked so often. "I know you are Jewish." Helena turned white, unable even to protest.

"Don't worry, don't worry," I said quickly, dropping the dress I was folding and reaching over to hold her by the shoulders and forcing her to look right at my face. "Don't worry, because I'm Jewish too."

Helena stopped and stared. Then a small smile started to creep onto her face. "But how do you know? Why do you say this?"

"Remember on the train coming here? You had a dream and spoke Yiddish. I heard you. I was the one who woke you." And so we laughed and hugged and cried, and swore to be friends and keep our secrets safe. We would talk sometimes about our families when we were sure no one would overhear us. But we didn't work together, and I still spent a lot of time with Wladek, and besides, shared secret or no, you had to be careful. Better not to get too close, I thought, to anyone.

And so the days passed, not unhappily. Maybe the war would be over soon, I would think, and then I could go and look for my family. Soon Mother and Father and Rivka and Ida and Dora and David and I—all of us would be together again, telling stories of how each of us had survived, laughing at how worried we had all been not knowing about each other. I thought about it a lot, just before falling off to sleep.

I thought about it too when everyone in the barracks got mail, letters and packages from friends and family back home, and I never got any. Their families might be in difficult circumstances in occupied or battle zones, but they weren't in labor camps or ghettoes or hiding or vanished, as Helena's and mine were. Helena's real name was Esther.

In fact it looked kind of funny that I was the only one who never got any letters or packages, suspiciously funny, so I began to write myself letters, mailing them so that they would be delivered to me when everyone else got their mail. Nobody looked too closely at the postmarks, and I would quickly tear up the envelope, throw it away, and read the letters aloud, letters that explained why they couldn't send any packages, no money or food or whatever, going on to tell them about my brother and three sisters, about how well they were all doing, how big they were growing, and how they couldn't wait until I came back home to tell them about all my adventures in Germany.

Sometimes I would cry for real when I read the letters, and the girls in the barracks would come over and share with me what little treasures they had. I didn't have to explain, they understood, I was lonely just as they were.

We heard stories now and then, mostly from the other girls, about camps for Jews, and even about gas chambers and crematoriums. They were told in a half-joking way, perhaps fantasies of anti-Semites. Nobody paid much attention to them.

But once while reading a newspaper in the barracks, I came upon a boast by Hitler. "If," he said, "I should find a Jew alive today in Germany, I would personally shake his hand and then I would let him go." I laughed a little within myself, and thought about it for a brief moment. Later on I tore it out and showed it to Helena/Esther, and we giggled together.

All this time Wladek kept coming, always bringing a treat or two, which I would often share with the other girls, but one day when I expected him to come, he didn't show up. The next day Lada came to tell me that Wladek had been arrested. It turned out that he did have a secret.

He was really a spy for the Polish underground, stationed there to report back on the conditions of Polish workers in Germany. Maybe they discovered his radio equipment, or maybe someone had turned him in. I never knew. He was just gone. Dead, perhaps.

The Gestapo came soon after to question me about him, but in truth I knew very little. We had always wanted it that way. They finished their questions and left me alone, and life went on.

In time, the bombs started to fall, the Allied saturation bombing was on, which the British thought was going to affect the course of the war so much, and which never really did.

It was early summer 1943, and I had been in the factory for about eight months. Life had settled into a routine. One day I suggested to a Polish girl I knew in the barracks that we try to leave. We had some money, I could speak adequate German, and if we could get out on the street, we could go to another town just like any other Germans. As Polish laborers, of course. We couldn't travel without papers, but if no one asked, we wouldn't need any, would we?

But before we left, I said, we had to go shopping to get some new clothes, maybe a hat. If we were going on the train like German ladies, we had to look nice.

The other girl thought that made sense. It sounded like an adventure, but that day, before we could go on our shopping expedition, we heard that Helena/Esther had been arrested.

CHAPTER EIGHT

Descent

In truth I had always had a few doubts about Helena/Esther. She wasn't very bright, which was no crime, but under these circumstances, slow-wittedness could be mortally dangerous, and not just for her. But I had needed a friend and had confided in her, and now it was too late, and what would happen would happen.

That day I went to work with an uneasy feeling, a feeling of some ominous doom hanging over me. The thoughts of leaving the factory, of shopping for a new hat and clothes for my light-hearted adventure, vanished with the news of Esther's arrest. Now I dared not risk such an escapade. I felt as if I was being watched. I just tried to work day by day, hour by hour, without calling any attention to myself.

But when a few days later I looked in my laboratory window and saw several Gestapo men approaching my wing of the factory, I was not surprised. They are coming for me now, I thought. There were hundreds of workers in that part of the factory, but I knew they were coming for me. I guess I had always felt it would happen sometime, like waiting for the German *Aktion* in Strzyzow all those years! It will come—the only question is when. But still, the hope always remained that the war might be over first, before they found me.

I took a last look around the lab. The white walls, the marble sink, the big curved windows. It really was quite beautiful, so clean and spare and graceful. I will miss it, I thought. Whatever comes now will not be as nice.

Two Gestapo men were talking with the lab supervisor, the one who had given me the sandwiches. He seemed surprised by what they were saying, as he looked first at me and then back at the Gestapo men.

Finally they came over to me and asked me if my name was Kazimiera Lukashuk, and I said, "Yes, of course it is." They said I had to go with them. I nodded. The supervisor stared on after us, looking puzzled, almost embarrassed.

Being driven to the police station in the back of a car, I felt oddly calm. Whatever happens, I kept thinking, I'm going to stick by my story. If they kill me, they kill me. I don't know what they know, or how they know it. Maybe it was the Jewish girl. Maybe it was just more questions about Wladek. Whatever it is, whether they kill me because I'm lying or they kill me because they know I'm Jewish, it's all the same. I'm dead either way, but I'm not going to make it easy for them.

One was ugly, and one was big and fat, and as we drove, I kept getting calmer and calmer. I was in so deep now, there was no way out, and that focussed me wholly on the moment. There would be no past, no future, no regrets, no second chances. One time only.

We stopped, and I was taken to a Gestapo jail, an ordinary room where I was left alone the rest of the day and night, except for one meal and one chance to relieve myself. They wanted me to get tired mentally, to lose my resolve, to become afraid.

Perhaps that was the idea, softening me up. The Germans had these things down to a science. I tried instead to think of other things, of my family, of Urszula and her mother's piano, anything to avoid despair or the weakening of my will. Clearly, I was no Helena/Esther. I was going to stick to my story.

The next morning, without breakfast of course, I was taken into a room with two Gestapo men for questioning. One, I quickly realized, was more of a translator. He spoke German and Polish fluently. The other was clearly the expert at interrogation, a real German.

He spoke to me first in German, but I wasn't going to fall for that. They could kill me, but I wasn't stupid enough to help them do it. If it was harder for them to use Polish through a translator, good. Better still, they didn't know I could understand them when they talked to each other.

"I don't understand anything you are saying," I said in Polish looking at the questioner, then at the translator.

The interrogator understood that well enough. He nodded to the translator. "Do you want me to speak Polish to you?" the man said.

"Yes."

"Are you Kazimiera Lukashuk?"

"Yes."

"Aren't you Jewish?"

"No."

The German just watched me while the other asked the questions.

"Did you know the girl Helena who was arrested the other day?" Ah, now I knew why I had been brought in here.

"Certainly, she lived in the barracks with me. How could I not know her?" Knowing just what had gone wrong made me feel bolder. It's only my life. They can only kill me once.

"But didn't you tell her you were Jewish?" he went on almost pleasantly, as if he were trying to clear up some minor discrepancy in his records. He was very good at his job, that German, but for me it was not my job, but my life. I had to be better.

"Jewish? Of course not." I produced what I hope was a smile. "Why would I tell her I'm Jewish?"

"She said you did."

"Then she's lying."

We went on like this for some time. Questions over and over without getting any further. All they have, I kept thinking, is the word of that Helena/Esther, her word against mine. If I were a man, it would be different. But how can they really prove that a girl is a Jew? Of course, there was my friendship with Wladek. That didn't make me a Jew either, but it could be one more thing to hold against me. In Poland or the Ukraine, they would just kill me anyway. I'd be dead already, none of this formality of an interrogation. But in Germany, they go through proper procedures, and killing many foreign workers would not look good. They needed us.

Then a third man came into the room, a German like the other, but one who spoke Polish as well as the translator. He muttered privately to the others, then turned to me.

"You say your name is Kazimiera Lukashuk?" he asked in Polish?

"Yes." All this over again.

"And you were born in Wlodimierz?"

"Yes."

"And you lived there until you separated from your parents when Wlodimierz came temporarily under Russian control?"

"Yes." Wlodimierz was about 50 kilometers east of Hrubieszow, east of the Bug River.

"Well, as you know, it is now under German control. We

have made some inquiries, and I have the response with me. Now, Kazimiera Elisa Lukashuk of Wlodimierz was killed in a bombing raid on Lublin two years ago. The records confirm it."

He put his folder down, but not so near that I could read it. My brain raced. It could have been a bluff. The girl was dead, so why argue with them? The Germans were famous for their records, their dossiers. God knows they probably knew more about the real Kazimiera than I did. Besides, if I asked to see the information, they would know I knew German. I looked at this third interrogator, calm and professional, gazing at me blandly.

When caught in a lie, the only hope is sometimes another lie. Kazimiera Lukashuk was dead? Then I would be somebody else, not Rosalia certainly but somebody they'd have a tougher time checking on.

"You are right," I said after a long pause. "I was lying. I am not Kazimiera Lukashuk. My real name is Kazimiera Wisniewska and I am from Pinsk." They stared at me unblinking.

"My papers were lost when the German soldiers came through. All my family was killed." On inspiration, I salted this story with a grain of truth.

"I got these papers on the black market in Lublin. It was the only way I could get here."

Pinsk, I knew, was also under German control, but it was part of occupied White Russia along the path of heavy fighting, on the way to and back from Moscow. It had been in the newspapers with maps. Records from there, I figured, might not be as easy to come by as those from the Reichskommissariat Ukraine, which supervised the Wlodimierz region. Or so I hoped.

It was a guess, a chance I took. When your life depends it,

a lot of things occur to you that might not otherwise. If they don't, you don't end up writing about them.

They continued to question me for a few hours, but I stuck fast to this new story. I clearly wasn't the woman who I had said I was, but I might be who I now said I was. My story wasn't particularly unusual, and holding false papers, while a crime, didn't make me a Jew. They still had only the word of a confessed Jew for that.

I could imagine them thinking they could keep me there until they had checked out this new story, but that could take weeks, maybe months. And Jew or Pole or Russian even, I was only a young girl, not worth making a big fuss about.

Toward the end of the day, when it became clear they weren't going to get any further with me, the three conferred in German. They looked disgusted and bored.

Finally, the third one, clearly the senior interrogator, spoke. "We are never going to find out what she really is. Let's stop wasting our time. Let's just get rid of her. Send her to Auschwitz. Let her die there."

He said this in German, and of course I understood all of it. I felt relieved. They were not going to kill me immediately. And who knows, I thought, what it would be like there in that Auschwitz place. It might not be so bad.

I was kept in jail in Leverkusen for two days after the interrogation. They would not allow me to go back to my barracks to get any of my things, and everything I had, except what was literally on my back, was stripped from me.

From Leverkusen, I was taken by train to Hannover in the company of several other prisoners and a few guards. It was a trip of some 250 kilometers, lasting most of the day, with expected delays to let troop and munitions trains through. We traveled in a normal passenger train compartment, not much different from the train I had taken into Germany in the first place. As long as we were traveling in Germany, appearances had to be maintained. Things still had to look civilized.

My jail in Hannover, however, was my first contact with a real cell. It was cold, damp, and ugly. I was kept with several other women, mostly Polish, mostly older, imprisoned for various political "crimes," accused of sabotage, a husband discovered in the Partisan resistance, insulting a German officer, and so on.

After a few days, enough prisoners were accumulated to warrant a transport to Berlin. Again, a normal train with regular seats, another 250 kilometers back the way I had first come.

The jail in Berlin was much better than the one in Hannover, and I began to develop some friendships in this strange but intimate community. I felt more open, more comfortable here than I had ever felt in Leverkusen. Of course I was still hiding, still not being myself as a Jew, but not hiding so much as before. I was already a prisoner. They already knew some of my secrets. There was less to be revealed, less to be afraid of. Somehow discovery made me feel less at risk. Relatively speaking, there was now less to lose.

Soon I developed a warm friendship with a Gypsy woman on her way to the camps. This woman could tell fortunes with cards, and she taught me how to do it. We would practice with the other prisoners or with each other. Neither one of us really put too much stock in it. It was a way to pass the time. We used to look solemnly at the cards, and then tell the person whose fortune we were reading that she would soon be going on a long journey. It was a good joke. None of us, we knew, would be in the Berlin jail for very long.

Also I got to know a Polish boy, who was a trustee of the

jail. This meant that he had some privileges not granted to other prisoners. He told me he was going to take care of me, bring me some extra food, dish out to me the best part of the soup, the bones and meat which had settled at the bottom of the serving pot. But I wondered if like Wladek, he too would one day just disappear. I figured I wouldn't be there long enough to find out, and I just went along.

He was able to extend favors from the kitchen to our guards as well. They were mostly poor women, hardly in much better shape than the prisoners. He managed to bring them some extra bread, and spent extra time talking with me, even giving me letters he had written. Another prisoner started writing poetry about us. Between the food and the card playing and the letters and poems, the jail became a warm, almost homey place, and I remember hoping "the cards" were wrong, that we all might stay there for a while yet.

But one day a few weeks later, the orders came. I was to leave the next day. That night I stayed up crying and laughing and talking to everyone. It was very sad. We left Berlin in a conventional train again, but when we reached the Polish border, that too finally changed. It was October 1943 by then, and cold, but we were ordered outside in the bitter chill and told to wait by soldiers armed with submachine guns. Then a few hours later, we were herded into a bare wooden box car and packed together, 60 or 100 to a car. We were no longer in Germany. The pretense of civilization could be dropped.

We couldn't sit or even lean, except against one another. The only ventilation was a slit window. Soon the stench of packed bodies and excrement was unbearable. No food, no water, you couldn't sleep, you could hardly breathe. Now, I thought, they have finally made me into an animal.

It got colder, and some of the older people died. They died while standing up. There was no room to fall down.

I thought about jumping off the train. The door would open only from time to time to throw out the slop buckets. People weren't allowed out. They couldn't relieve themselves. They would be killed the very moment they tried to leave the car.

When we stopped in a Polish town, to refuel the train I suppose, and the door was opened and we put out our hands to beg for a piece of bread or a cup of water, the Polish peasants by the siding gave us instead stones and sand, threw it at us, and laughed.

They must have thought we were Jews. I gave up thoughts of jumping, weak, alone, into this sea of medieval hatred. I wouldn't get far that way. No, whatever Auschwitz was, I would have to face it. There was no escape now.

Every minute was like a month. No way to tell day from night. It was probably two days. People kept dying all around me, freezing to death. I made up my mind to live, and kept thinking of my family, my Mother and Father, and vowed that I would live to tell them what I had gone through.

When they finally opened the doors and let us out, about half of those in each car were dead. I looked around numbly. The railroad tracks ended here, a spur line apparently. SS men swarmed everywhere, carrying submachine guns and accompanied by big dogs, as if, after our terrible trip, any of us had the strength to resist. But then, maybe the guns weren't for resisters, because when a prisoner was too weak to walk, he or she was simply shot.

Ahead of us was a large sinister gate with an arch above it, and a sign in German, "Arbeit Macht Frei," "Work Makes You Free." I didn't believe the motto, but at least now I could believe this was a labor camp. Nearby was a huge mound of bags and suitcases, and boxes of clothing. Any of us who still possessed something had to deposit it on the pile. Behind us, men in prison garb began to drag the dead bodies from the cars and make another pile of them.

And while all this was going on, music was playing. Eerily, a whole orchestra of inmates stood nearby, producing waltzes, mazurkas, polkas, and other lilting melodies.

Our group was quickly segregated by sex, the women on one side, and the men on the other. We were all "political" or "social" prisoners, not Jews. I was led away with the other young women to a large shower area. Real showers. We didn't yet know about the other kind.

We crowded in, the doors were closed, and water came out. We were grateful for the opportunity to get clean. Then we were deloused. Our heads were shaved. And finally, we were given new outfits, uniform dresses with broad blue and white stripes and a patch. Mine was a red triangle with a "P" in the middle. Later I was told that meant "political."

We were then led over to have our numbers tattooed on our forearms. Mine was 64062, a low number, a Polish number. Later we would be segregated again, by ability to work. But for now, we were simply led off to our barracks.

I had heard of such places for years now, of course, but I think I never really believed they existed. Just stories, I'd thought, to scare the Jews. But now I saw the signs and the electric fence that surrounded everything, and the high watchtowers every hundred meters with guards stationed in each one, and I knew. It was true. This was a death camp. Send her to Auschwitz, he had said. Let her die there.

CHAPTER NINE

Oswiecim

Jack and I spent three days in Krakow, Poland's ancient capital and oldest city, much older than Warsaw and for centuries the intellectual center of Polish life. Its oldest university is here, as are many learned societies, academies, museums, historical monuments, and art treasures. But we were not there as scholars or even tourists. We were on a trip to a more recent past.

Krakow is the closest large city to Oswiecim, Polish for Auschwitz, and we were on our way back to the camp. Now I didn't want to go. I was afraid to, afraid of what I might find in that place. But I had to go. I owed it to Kazimiera Wisniewska. So one morning, my stomach as tense as a board, we set out.

Now, in 1985, you could reach the camp by car. When we pulled up before the gate, there was the same lying sign, "Arbeit Macht Frei." Everything looked neat, clean, official, well-kept, empty of people. But nearby was the same end-of-the-line railroad stop where the cars had been unloaded. I recognized the places where the SS had milled about, where the luggage had been piled up. Over there was where that unreal orchestra had made its music.

Oświęcim — Brzezinka, dn. 24.08. 1987 r.

L. dz.IV-8520-168/ 2510 /87

**PAŃSTWOWE
MUZEUM
OŚWIĘCIM
BRZEZINKA**

NBP OŚWIĘCIM
KONTO 718-92-7

CENTRALA TELEF.
20-21 — 20-24

MUZEUM CZYNNE
CODZIENNIE
W GODZ. 8-15
OPRÓCZ
PONIEDZIAŁKÓW
I DNI
POŚWIĄTECZNYCH

PRZYJAZD
ZWIEDZAJĄCYCH
NALEŻY
WCZEŚNIEJ
ZGŁOSIC

Pani

Rose T o r e n

265 SO. Maple DR. B.H. California

U.S.A.

Państwowe Muzeum Oświęcim-Brzezinka stwierdza
niniejszym, że WISZNIEWSKA Alice, ur. 4.10.1923
Pińsk, została przywieziona do hitlerowskiego obozu
koncentracyjnego Auschwitz w Oświęcimiu transportem
z Lublina i zarejestrowana w obozie dnia 3.10.1943 r.
oraz oznaczona numerem więźniarskim 64062, który został
wymienionej więźniarce wytatuowany na przedramieniu
lewej ręki. --
Pod datą 16.08.1944 r. wymieniona więźniarka wymieniona jest w aktach Instytutu Higieny. W KL Auschwitz
przebywała do stycznia 1945 r. a następnie zbiegła
z trasy ewakuacyjnej. Innych danych o wymienionej
Muzeum nie posiada. -----------------------------------

Podstawa informacji:
Numerowy wykaz transportów; Akta Insytutu Higieny;
ankieta. --

DYREKTOR
z up.
/mgr Kazimierz Smoleń/

TI/TI

*A letter from the Director of the National Museum in Auschwitz
confirming the presence and number of the author in the camp.*

A fragment of the records listing the inmates at Auschwitz. Note the name of the author, highlighted in the lower part of the column.

Jack took my arm and we walked through the gate. A building that had been erected since my time stood just inside, officially labelled "Panstwowe Muzeum Oswiecim-Brzezinka," State Museum of Auschwitz-Birkenau. We went inside and were greeted by the curator whose name had been given us by a friend. He had been expecting us, and although he didn't go so far as to kiss my hand the way Poles often do, he was very cordial.

"I'm Kazimiera Alice Wisniewska," I said, using the name I had invented. "I was here from 1943 to 1945."

113

"Ah yes, if you will wait just a few minutes." He vanished into a back region, and shortly after reappeared with a typed certificate. "The State Museum of Auschwitz-Birkenau hereby affirms that WISNIEWSKA Alice, born 4.10.23 Pinsk was transported to the Hitlerite concentration camp on the day 3.10.1943."

So I was a bona fide inmate, and had a paper to prove it. And then, for some reason, perhaps because I wanted to be known as an inmate under my own name, I told him what it was.

"Rosalia Orenstein. I am a Jew."

His manner hardened, like a pond freezing over. He remained perfectly courteous, but now he was no longer cordial.

"I see. Well then, will you require a guide to the various areas?"

"No," I said. "I know my way only too well."

His farewell handshake was limp, uninterested.

The Birkenau 2 Death Camp was located near the town of Oswiecim, in southern Poland, west of Krakow. To it were brought those to be imprisoned or eliminated for one reason or another. Those Jews taken directly from the trains to the gas chambers were not given uniforms or identifying badges. They were not statistically registered by name or number either, but went anonymously to their deaths. These made up some 90% of those entering Auschwitz.

The remaining 10%, those selected as the fittest and most able to work for a brief time, were given yellow stars as distinguishing badges, but were mixed in the barracks with other categories of prisoners. They were also set aside by

The slogan over the entranceway to Auschwitz:
"Work makes you free."

their lack of certain privileges, such as receiving or sending mail, or receiving packages of food.

These Jews came from all areas under German influence or control, Poland, the Soviet Union—primarily the Ukraine, Byelorussia, Lithuania, Latvia, Estonia, Germany itself, Austria, Belgium, Holland, France, Luxembourg, the Protectorate (Western Czechoslovakia), Slovakia, Hungary, Yugoslavia, Greece, and Norway.

Political prisoners were identified by red triangles. These included Resistance fighters and their families, suspected saboteurs, and others like me, unknown, or simply "problems." Other categories were Jehovah's Witnesses wearing purple triangles, homosexuals wearing pink triangles, professional gamblers, pimps, those who shirked work, gigolos, and other undesirables wearing black stars, habitual criminals wearing green triangles, and Gypsies as well as other assorted "enemies of the Reich" wearing brown triangles. All of us were neatly classified.

Birkenau 2 had been opened in October of 1941, an expansion of a much smaller labor and detention camp opened earlier that year. It had been designed to hold approximately 130,000 prisoners at one time. The gas chambers were opened in the spring of 1942, and an estimated 3,500,000 people, the majority of them European Jews, were killed there. Most of these went directly from the train disembarkation to the underground chambers, which were disguised as showers.

The camp was divided into three main areas, B 1, the southern section; B 2, the middle; and B 3, the northern section. Area B 1A, the eastern half of the southern section, was made a women's camp in the summer of 1942. B 1B, the western half, also became a women's camp in the summer of 1943, after B 1A became full. My barracks was in B 1A, only a short distance from the end of the special railroad spur entering the camp.

Two gas chambers and adjacent crematoriums were within sight and smell of where I lived and where I worked. From my window, I could look out, oh, perhaps 10 meters away, and see the naked victims being herded to the "showers," the other kind.

The gas chambers were large structures, the main portion of which was underground. Each was 340 feet long and 170 feet wide. They had the capacity of some 2,000 murders at a time, an estimated yearly capacity of 1,000,000. The crematoriums had 15 ovens, which disposed of the bodies after the gold teeth had been removed. The acrid stench permeated the air of the camp day and night.

The day after our arrival at Auschwitz came our segregation by age and job. Young Jews, men and women, and those who fitted into the other categories of prisoners, such as politicals like me, were assigned work. This too would determine how long you might live. Given the rations, heavy work almost invariably meant death in a short time. You could see that right away.

I waited in line, and moved toward the woman who would give us our job assignment. She was one of the young Jewish capos, whose name I learned was Stella. Later she would be hanged after a failed escape attempt. When I got to know her, I knew my life depended on the job I got.

"I'm so tired," I said. "Can you give me a good job?"

"What do you know how to do?" she answered.

"What do you want me to know?" We both knew what I meant.

"Can you make sweaters?" she asked after a moment. She spoke pretty good Polish, and I answered in the same language, careful not to sound too educated. You never know what can turn somebody against you.

"Of course I do. Please," I said, "give me a job in strickereien making sweaters."

"You are sure you know how?" she asked again. Her job and life could also be at stake.

"Definitely!" I answered. I knew about as much about knitting sweaters as I did about driving a tractor. I had hardly even held a knitting needle in my hand, but I had to get that job. Clean, indoors, you might survive doing that.

Stella said, "OK, you go to the strickereien." I thanked her and moved on.

Then I was assigned a barracks near the strickereien. I

My bunk in Auschwitz.

would sleep on a bunk with five other women, a bunk made of wood just like the floor, with five other bunks above it. Three such layers of bunks were in each row, and there were two rows divided by a narrow corridor. About 200 women lived in each barracks.

The bunks were so crowded, I quickly realized, that if you woke up in the night and wanted to turn over, you'd have to wake up someone else in your bunk to do so. I soon learned to be a sound sleeper.

The strickereien consisted of 20 or so rows of chairs and tables at which two to four women worked. Our first job was to unravel wool from the piles of sweaters given to us. These came from clothing confiscated throughout the occupied

Reich, but principally they came from Auschwitz. The closest source was the clothing of those killed daily in the gas chambers.

When entering the camp, most prisoners, especially those who had been taken from the ghettoes or rounded up in the *Actions* who thus could anticipate the move long in advance, wore their best and warmest clothes, just as I had at Miaczyn. Others if arrested unexpectedly, like me in Leverkusen, wore just what they had on at the time.

Those who had anticipated their capture, in the time immemorial tradition, had quite often sewed small valuables, gold coins, jewelry, and the like, into the lining of their clothing. Our first job was to retrieve these little treasures before we unravelled the sweaters. I was always afraid I might find something I would recognize from my family or friends, but I never did, thank God.

Beautiful items, antique jewelry worth a lifetime of savings, treasures of the Jews of Hungary and Romania and Poland and the rest of Europe, daily passed through our fingers. We were warned that failure to turn in any of these items would result in immediate execution, and very seldom, if ever, would any of us take the risk. I never did. I didn't want money or jewels, I wanted to see my family again. Besides, what good was a diamond or gold bracelet in Auschwitz. Better a piece of bread. It satisfies now, and leaves no evidence for later.

It was a matter of life and death, for me and for Stella, to learn sweater-making fast. I was able to do this by starting with unravelling the old sweaters we got, and then as fast as I could, learning to make sweaters by copying the other workers. Luckily, I got away with it.

Sweaters, in fact, were more valuable than jewelry. They at least kept you warm, and could be unobtrusively traded for other commodities. It's funny too. Even today, I don't like jewelry. It seems to me like such a waste, such a false hope of security.

Our typical day began with the morning roll call, in German, the *Appell*. We always stood outside in the cold, at 5:00 o'clock in the morning, in the dark, in the snow, and in wooden shoes with no stockings and just a thin dress, as they checked for the sick, dead, and missing. At times my feet froze, turned black and blue, and swelled up.

They counted the standing bodies, and if everyone was there, we returned to the barracks. If someone was missing, we were called off by our numbers to see who it was. Names were never used, except by prisoners to each other. I was Kazia, of course, short for Kazimiera. Last names were seldom used, even by prisoners to each other.

If someone was missing, we had to stand there until she was found or accounted for. Once when an escape was attempted by two young capos who had managed to steal an officer's car, we were kept standing there all day, and through the night until the next morning. Fortunately, this was in the springtime, or we all would have died.

Another time when an escapee was caught, instead of going directly to work, we were all first marched to a central compound to watch him being hanged.

After roll call, we usually returned to the barracks for breakfast, a few pieces of bread and some warm liquid. Lunch and dinner were the same.

Our guards were a mixture of Germans and Poles, and Jewish capos. Capos were often the cruelest of the lot, worse than the Germans. Of course, they had the most to lose. They were part of the dead, really, only their bodies were still warm.

A few weeks after my arrival at Auschwitz, my menstrual

The crematorium in Auschwitz, revisited in 1985.

periods stopped and never returned while I was there. I thought then there was something in the food to cause it, since so few others seemed to have periods. Now I realize it was the undernourishment plus the tension and fear.

Yes, we knew about Dr. Mengele and his experiments, although it did not affect us as ordinary working prisoners. His victims were taken off the trains from the fresh arrivals, beautiful young boys and girls. Those in the camp for any length of time were not in good enough condition to undergo the medical experimentation, not pretty enough to be desired for the brothels.

Death was commonplace in the camp. If you didn't get shot or hanged for some infraction of the rules, you succumbed to cold, hunger, disease, despair. I nearly did myself. People who died were loaded onto death carts, and dragged to the central compound, a big empty space in the camp like a town square, and dumped. Often I saw hundreds of naked bodies piled up there, and trucks coming to be loaded with them. Prisoners would throw the bodies onto the trucks like garbage. Human beings thrown away like trash.

After a while, we got so used to it we paid little attention to anything that didn't directly concern our personal survival. We wanted to live, and that's what we thought about. Watching through the window of the strickereien, we saw women and children pushing to get into the gas chambers. They just got off those horrible trains, and they'd been told they were to have showers. Naturally, they pushed and shoved, eager to be first. Nobody ever went out to tell them what was going to happen. We all saw the procession pass by every day, and nobody said a word. If you did, you would be killed, so you were silent, dumb, numb, and you lived another day.

Becoming an official state museum had not changed what Auschwitz really was. Jack and I looked around. A few trees had been allowed to seed themselves and grow up between the double fences of barbed wire. Only an occasional guard's watch tower was still left. But it remained a grey, flat, windswept place, bleak in its tragic memories, silent in its emptiness.

Many of the barracks which had housed such a packed overcrowding of humanity had been allowed to fall down, or had been deliberately burned. Here and there we saw the jumbled foundations. One set of gas chambers had been destroyed by the Germans before the oncoming Red Army had overtaken them.

The remains of the gas chambers at Auschwitz.

In several places, we saw rotting and abandoned death carts, the kind on which human corpses were hauled to the "town square."

What seemed most different to me was the emptiness. I remembered Auschwitz chiefly for its people, the hapless swarms of inmates and gas chamber victims, for the brutal Death's Head squad guards and their guns and their dogs, and now—no one.

Despite my boast to the curator, I had trouble getting my bearings. We wandered about for a while, not sure where we were. Despite how familiar it looked, everything seemed so strange. Perhaps it was the missing buildings. I couldn't find my own barracks, and soon I began to wonder. It could have been among those that had fallen down or been burned. The bouquet of flowers that we had bought in Krakow grew hot in my hand from tension and frustration.

Then suddenly I recognized one building. "That's the place where we took showers," I said. We hurried over. Yes, this was the shower room, and over here was where our heads had been shaved, the delousing, the tattooing, the new prison uniforms. I knew where I was now.

The strickereien must be, yes, over there. The large room which had held so many women whose busy fingers had worked, worked, worked over the piles of sweaters, was nearly empty, but from its windows you could see the same gas chambers, the same crematoriums. Just over there, in a space the width of an American street, the new arrivals, already stripped of their clothes and valuables, had pushed and shoved to be the first into the "showers."

I turned away. My barracks. I had to find my barracks. It couldn't be far from here.

CHAPTER
TEN

64062

As I passed the end of my first year in Auschwitz, in the autumn of 1944, the camp was overrun with an epidemic of typhus. Illness, particularly a debilitating illness like typhus, was our worst fear, next to death itself. If you could still work, you might live. If not, you were worthless, already dead.

One morning I awoke delirious, with a high fever and a dry, burning feeling in my mouth, nose and lungs. I tried to get out of my bunk and couldn't. I was terrified.

They took me to the infirmary after roll call, still delirious. Patients were placed there only two to a bunk, the head of one by the toes of the other, like a valet, the jack in a deck of playing cards.

It was snowing outside, but I was hot, burning up. I kept thinking, "If I could just go outside and lie down in the snow and cool off. Just for a little while. If only I could get up out of the bunk."

I begged a Polish woman near me to help me go out and lie in the snow, and maybe to eat some of it. The snow would be so cool and refreshing.

"Not yet," said the woman. Not yet time to die. Soon enough, perhaps. But not yet.

I slept instead, and when I woke, I wondered if I had said anything to reveal myself in my delirious sleep. Like Helena/Esther on the train to Koln. But nobody said anything or looked at me differently. Maybe my secret identity was still safe.

Then I looked around at this house of the dead in this kingdom of death, thinking, "Safe? Alive, anyway, for now." I felt the other girl, who had shared my bunk since I'd first been brought in. I wanted to turn over, but the girl was in the way. I tapped her again to ask her to move. No response. I shook her harder. Still no response. Finally I raised myself up enough to look down the bed at her face. She looked dead. I signaled the guard, who checked on the girl.

"Finished," he said, and had her taken away. I fell back into a deep sleep brought on by the exertion, wondering if this had been another delirious dream. It was hard to tell the difference now.

The infirmary was divided into two sides, a Jewish side and a side for the others, where I'd been placed. The day here still began with the morning roll call, but only those on the Jewish side had to answer to it. The others, if they were too weak, could stay in bed. But if anyone on the Jewish side could not stand for the *Appell,* she was taken from there to the gas chambers.

The next morning was the worst. I woke up so delirious I couldn't figure out where I was. It wasn't the barracks, I knew that. Not enough people. And too quiet. Strangely quiet. Wherever it was, I was hot, burning up again. I had to go out and lie down in the snow. Had to, or I would die.

I looked around and saw a group being readied to go someplace, someplace outside, I was sure. Why else would people be getting up? To go to the bathroom? But not in a group like that.

So I got up too and wandered over to that side to go with them. If I got outside, it would be all right. Just for a moment, to lie down in the snow. So cool and refreshing.

But just before the group of women was led out, a Polish woman came over to me. "Where are you going, my child?" she said quietly.

I couldn't say. I couldn't even hear the question. I had gone deaf from the fever that night.

The woman led me back over to my bunk, on the non-Jewish side. The others were led out, and soon after, gassed. As I again fell into a fitful sleep, the smell of the burning flesh from the mordant black smokestacks of the crematoriums filled my nostrils.

When I started to recover, I soon realized how close I had come to death. And I began to keep an eye on the others and how they acted, those on the other side, who soon would be led out with no one to save them. When the meals came, the soup and bread, no matter how sick they were, no matter how sure they were they would soon be dead, they all ate ravenously, like animals, gobbling down the small portions, fighting for an extra piece of bread. Food was now. Death was later. It was the way of life and death in the camp.

I pitied them, and I was happy then that I was not recognized as a Jew. Happy to be Kazia, not Rosalia. Rosalia, now, would be dead.

When the fever finally broke, my hearing returned. I hungered for conversation again, more than for food or drink. A new Polish girl in a neighboring bunk watched me for a while, and then came up and sat beside me.

We began to talk, of this and that, nothing special. Then the girl, whose name was Anna, said, "Look, I have a feeling I will never survive this place."

She was young and pretty, even as tired and sick as she was. "What do you mean?" I said. "Of course you will."

"No, I do not think so." She said it as if she were checking over a grocery bill, one which just did not add up. "But if you should make it, there is something I want you to do. Go to my parents, and tell them they should not wait for me."

I tried to reassure her some more, but finally promised to do what she asked, and she promised the same for me if I did not make it.

Shortly after, Anna died. Her face and promise burned into my memory. This was one promise I would keep, if I lived.

In a few days I recovered enough to return to my own barracks. With my shaven head and emaciated body I only weighed about 40 kilos by then. I must have looked like a vastly undernourished adolescent boy. But I was still alive.

And I still filled my nights with thoughts of my parents, and the dream of being together with them all again, to tell them how I had suffered. To tell stories of how we all had suffered and survived. I knew what was going on, now. You would have to be blind not to see it. You could even smell it. They were killing Jews, burning Jews by the thousands every day. If they were doing it here, they were doing it all over.

But not me, not yet. And not my family. Those others all might die, I'd think, but my parents are alive someplace, and I shall live to see them again. To tell them how I have suffered and to have them comfort me.

Yes, I would talk to them a lot, in my dreams and in my imagination. Long involved conversations. It helped make the time pass. It kept me alive.

Once we had located the strickereien, it was not hard to find my barracks. We walked in, and there it was just as I remembered it, except for the people. The bunks with a brick pier at either end, strong enough to support five wooden plank bunks and the 30 bodies they contained, the crumbling floor, the inadequate stove, the long central aisle.

The monument at Auschwitz in memory of six million Jews.

*I looked about the room, touched the hard sur-
faces of the bunks, and sniffed. Faint across the
decades came the scents of this time and place. Or
were they just the scents of memory?*

"Which bunk was yours?" Jack asked.

"This one."

*To make certain, I checked by glancing out the
nearby window. Yes, this was mine. Marysia had slept
next to me here, and while keeping each other company we had gossiped and giggled, momentarily
oblivious to the horrors.*

Our driver had followed us on our wanderings.

Now he stepped forward, pulling out his pocket knife, and carefully carved in the wood: "64062. Kazimiera Wisniewska."

I laid the flowers on my bunk, for Marysia and Kazia.

CHAPTER ELEVEN

Death March

Marysia and I shared more than a bunk. We were two of the four women at our work table in the strickerein. The others were Mrs. Mikolajczyk and Mrs. Dlugoszowska.

Mrs. Mikolajczyk was an important woman. Soon after the Nazi blitzkrieg victory in Poland, a government-in-exile had been set up in France, headed by Gen. Wladyslaw Sikorski, with Stanislaw Mikolajczyk as his deputy. There they gathered the remnants of Poland's Home Army. In June 1940, with the invasion of France and its rapid fall, the Polish government-in-exile left France for England. Most of them sailed on the liner *Batory*, one of the last Polish ships out of France. The same ship had carried virtually the last shipload of Jews out of Poland when I saw it leave Gydnia in the summer of 1939.

Mrs. Mikolajczyk stayed behind in France, on the assumption that in the time-honored tradition of political struggle, as a non-combatant, she would be left in peace. Not so to the Nazis. By 1943, Sikorski had died, and Mikolajczyk had become Premier of the exiled government in London. At the same time, after passing through a series of detention camps and jails, Mrs. Mikolajczyk ended up as a "political" in Auschwitz with a job in the strickereien.

At our work table, to which I returned after recovery from

typhus, a certain intimacy had developed among the four of us. Our work was relatively easy and demanded nothing of our minds. There was a lot of time to talk.

I was the "young girl" of the group, known of course only as "Kazia." Mrs. Dlugoszowska, an elegant Warsaw lady, had been imprisoned for harboring a political prisoner in her home. (If her family had not been as wealthy and influential as it was, she would have been summarily shot, she assured us calmly, and thus she would not have had "the pleasure of our delightful company.")

The fourth of the group was Marysia, who had become my best friend. Marysia was an uncommonly beautiful woman, looking much like the young Elizabeth Taylor, with a face like a porcelain doll. Although she had a glass eye, it did little to detract from her beauty. She had a fine spirit too, but was physically weak.

She was a little older than I, and had lived a rather sheltered life, coming from a respected upper-class Polish family in the region of Krakow. Her parents were in the Partisan underground, and her imprisonment was in lieu of theirs. Nothing in her early life had prepared her for Birkenau 2.

Toward the end, Marysia was allowed to receive packages sent from England by relatives in exile. She would share these with me. Most often she would simply give me the package and say, "Take what you want. Divide it however you want."

She seemed more ready to give up than I was, so while she shared food with me which helped me to live, I shared with her my burning will to survive and my dreams of a life after it was all over.

"You must block it out!" I would whisper to her fiercely when some ghastly sight seemed too inhuman to bear. "You must be hard and strong, and keep remembering that *you* are going to *survive*."

"I'm not as strong as you, Kazia."

"Yes you are! I'll make you as strong!"

Through the work and the friendships, my time in the sweater factory passed more easily. We all swore to each other that we would look the others up after the war. We all knew, had to believe, that we would survive.

Having so little else to do, we sometimes would get playful in our fantasies. "Let's get dressed up," one would say.

"Yes, let's go out."

"What shall we wear? Where shall we go?"

Then we'd search through the pile of sweaters, looking for one we liked. Then try it on, twirling like models for the others to judge. It was so hard to find something that went really well with broad vertical blue and white stripes, but we did our best.

Then came the jewelry. So much to choose from. "You know," I might say as we looked through the pile in front of us, "I think I'll take the little earrings. I'm too young to wear big ones. They wouldn't look right on me." The others would all think about this and finally agree. You didn't want to be garish now, did you?

And lastly, we had to decide where to go. Mrs. Mikolajczyk and Mrs. Dlugoszowska weighed the merits of the various Warsaw cafes. The glint in Mrs. Dlugoszowska's eye hinted that she didn't always go to them with Mr. Dlugoszowski. In Warsaw, much was allowed if you were discreet.

Marysia then discussed the various high spots of Krakow, while I might recall my days in Lublin. It was so hard, however, to decide what was right. In the end, a different spot for a different boy seemed best.

Yes, we had fun sometimes in the strickereien. And when the capo returned to check up on who was making all the noise, we would quickly shed the sweaters and jewelry, put our heads down, and get back to work.

Occasionally, we did consider taking some of the jewelry. "We're going to survive," someone said, "so why don't we take some diamonds and hide them someplace. They'll never miss them. When they go, we'll dig them up and we'll be rich." We talked about it quite seriously a few times, but we never did it. In the end, we were too afraid.

Others actually did try this scheme, and some got away with it and lived well on the proceeds after the war. Still others tried it and were shot.

People died in the camps without going to the gas chambers. Died of cold, hunger, disease, despair. Their bodies were carried to a big empty space, an open area in the camp, and dumped. Often we saw hundreds of naked bodies, and trucks coming along to be filled up with them. Prisoners would throw the bodies onto the trucks like garbage. You saw it and remembered, but if you wanted to live, to raise children some day, to survive even just that day, you blocked it out. I told Marysia, "Forget what you see."

Some days one thought only about getting up in the morning and surviving that day. One day they came into the barracks and took out a third of the people and killed them. There was a reason, I suppose, punishment for some infraction. No one knew or cared what it was. What mattered was that it wasn't you. That day it wasn't Rose or Marysia. That day, we survived.

Another day, Marysia and I were walking in the space between the barracks when I heard a word for the first time in the camp that meant death for me. It was my name, my real name.

"Rougea! Rougea!" Someone was calling me. I looked over quickly, hoping Marysia wouldn't notice. You trusted your friends with your life, up to a point. After that point, you trusted no one, unless you absolutely had to. Helena/Esther had taught me that.

Yet I knew the girl who was calling me. She was from Hrubieszow. We had gone to school together, a nice girl, a nice Jewish girl. She started to come over.

"Who are you talking to?" I said coldly as she approached. It stopped her in her tracks.

"To you, Rougea. Don't you know me?"

"My name is Kazimiera, and I do not know you." I tried surreptitiously to point to the red triangle on my dress, but the girl was too excited to notice.

"It's me, Rougea. Miriam, from Hrubieszow," she insisted almost desperately, and started walking toward me again.

"No!" I said even more sharply, still trying to avoid a dangerous scene. "No, you are mistaken. I'm not who you think I am. No please, we must go." I turned and walked on with Marysia, knowing that all the time the girl Miriam was staring after me, feeling her eyes boring into my back.

You had to survive, even if it meant not acknowledging a fellow Jew, a friend, a neighbor. We trusted no one, not this girl Miriam, not even Marysia. She too could be a spy, or let something slip accidentally. You did not take any risks you did not have to take. You followed that rule, or you died.

Do I remember the horrors? Children tortured, then gassed and burned? The faceless villains, ciphers in history?

I survived, after all, and I lived, not as a Jewess but as a Polish girl. And what did I think of the Jews then? Was I glad I was able to pretend not to be one? Yes. Was that shameful? Perhaps. But only those who were actually there, who experienced it all, should make that judgement.

I always wore the mask. It helped me to survive, but it wasn't me. Inside, in my heart and soul I knew that I was a Jew.

In the camp, it was almost impossible to keep clean. You were allowed to wash your dress every week or so, though without soap. You were dirty only half that week, but I wanted more, needed more, a clean dress, that was all. I traded a bit of bread, something from one of Marysia's food packages, plus a stolen sweater from work, for a second dress. It was just another prison garment of blue and white stripes, but it represented a chance to change my outfit regularly and be much cleaner.

That night, I hung both my dresses up on my bunk, feeling like a person of substance as I went to sleep. In the morning they were both gone, so I had nothing at all to wear, and had to borrow a dress for the *Appell*.

I began to cry. How could somebody do this to me? I couldn't stop crying like a baby, not for my Mother or my sisters. I was crying for a dress. Finally I said to myself that I must get out of this place soon, or it will be too late.

Later, I traded more food for another dress, and this one I used for a pillow every night. I learned my lesson. Other times I would steal a sweater from work to trade for more food, better soup which I got from a young Russian girl assigned to the kitchen. It was relatively easy to take a sweater. You just wore it back to the barracks from the strickereien. If you couldn't trade it, you wore it back the next morning and brought back a new one. I kept myself alive this way, and with me, Marysia. We helped each other to stay alive.

I had arrived in Auschwitz in the fall of 1943, and had already survived one winter. Now as the second winter in the camp approached, at the end of 1944, I really wondered if I would survive this one.

Christmas was coming, and with it maybe extra food in Marysia's packages. Maybe the Russians would come or the Americans. Maybe not. Something had to happen soon. The cold, disease, malnutrition, you couldn't beat the odds forever.

Then one night, we were all awakened by the German guards barking from the loudspeakers, rousing us in the barracks, "Achtung! Achtung!" Sirens on, dogs barking, soldiers massing.

No one knew what was happening. We all suspected and hoped that the Russians were finally coming.

"Take whatever you have," we were told. "You are leaving the camp." We hurriedly dressed, Marysia and I as always. It was the dead of winter, and the snow was deep. The smell of fear and panic came from the guards, and they didn't even take time to kill us. We were leaving instead, who knew where to? Who cared? Whatever happened, at least we would make it out of Auschwitz alive.

We were put in line standing in the snow, and counted. What else. Germans! Then we left into the night, cold and hungry women and men, already on the edge of death from malnutrition and exhaustion, ill-clad for a winter journey, urged on by the soldiers and the dogs, walking through the snow, thousands of us. Those who fell down were immediately shot. The sounds lingered in the frigid night air.

But Marysia and I remained on our feet and stayed together. We walked all through the night, holding onto each other for support. We didn't look back for the others, we didn't look to see who was shot. "How can we make it?" was all we thought about. How can we stay alive, now that it's almost over.

Marysia kept wanting to sit down, to give up. I wouldn't let her. We were too close to the end to give up now. Wherever we were going, whatever was going to happen to us, we were still alive, and there was a chance.

And from the houses we passed, people watched us. They

didn't say anything. Maybe they couldn't, maybe they didn't want to. I held tight to Marysia, my friend. I said, "Don't give up. We have suffered too much to give up now. Now we must live, we are young, we have a whole life ahead of us, and it's very close." She did not give up, that lovely, sweet, gentle woman. She marched on with me in the snow.

Later, this would come be known as the Auschwitz Death March.

> *We returned to Krakow, carrying my little certificate and putting Auschwitz with all its death and suffering behind us, or as much behind us as we ever could.*
>
> *I couldn't help but remember what the Gestapo interrogator had said. "Send her to Auschwitz, let her die there." Well, I didn't die. I'd probably outlived him, so that grim monument to inhumanity was not without a few triumphs as well as horrors.*
>
> *Had I carried out my promise to Anna, who had died in the infirmary? Yes. Just after the war, I went to the small town near Lodz where she lived, and sadly told her family about her death. We wept together. They said they were glad at least to know what had happened.*
>
> *But other obligations were not so easy to meet. There was the matter of finding my beloved Marysia.*

CHAPTER
TWELVE

Survival

Marysia and I walked on through the second day of the Death March. From time to time we heard the sounds of bombs and artillery. The fighting was close. We also heard the sharp bursts of shots from our guards, and the thuds in the snow. We were still a long way from being safe.

That night we finally stopped at a Polish farmhouse, commandeered by the Germans. Evening thankfully came early in the Polish winter. The peasant family on the farm brought us all some hot soup. I don't think anything in my life ever tasted quite so good.

Then everyone found a place to bed down. Marysia and I climbed up into the hayloft. Exhausted though we were, we slept restlessly.

"You know," I said to Marysia finally, "if we go on, we will surely die. Either we die on the march, we fall down and they shoot us, or we reach Germany and they will kill us there."

"What else can we do?"

"We can stay here. If they kill us here or there, what difference does it make? At least here, we'll die warm."

"This is not like you, Kazia, to give up, to talk of dying." Then she stopped. She must have seen the look in my eye.

"See, we can hide under the hay," I urged. "Maybe they

won't find us. I think we can make it this way. Please, Marysia, stay with me."

Marysia thought for a moment or two. "I will," she answered finally. "I'll stay with you here. I don't think I'd live very long in Germany. If they find us, they kill us. If not, we have a chance."

"Remember," I added, "they're close, the Russians. A few more days and we'll be safe. We have to try, we're so close."

We slept and turned for the remainder of the night, until the sounds of the Germans getting ready down below woke us up. We burrowed deeper into the hay and waited and listened, trying not to breathe. We heard some shots and the sounds of dogs barking. Someone climbed the ladder part way and then went down. More noises, awful noises of death, and then a stillness.

We waited until mid-day, and then decided we'd risk it. "We have to go down," I said. All had been quiet for hours.

"What if they're still there," whispered Marysia. "I don't think they are. The Russians are too close. Those guards didn't look very hard for us the first time. They just wanted to leave here quickly. If you want I will go first, and you can wait safely here. If I'm caught, I'll say I was alone. No one will know the difference."

"No," she shook her head firmly. "If you go, then I go with you. But what about the peasant family? What if they turn us in?"

"I don't think they will. Remember the soup? They knew who we were." I rubbed my patch, the red triangle.

"I guess you're right," Marysia said finally, and we went down together.

Down on ground, everyone was gone except the dead lying still in the snow. We hugged each other. Then we saw a man standing there watching us. It was the Polish farmer. We watched each other for a moment. Marysia began to speak.

"Please, I am a Polish woman with my friend. We were in prisons for no reason. I used to live not far from here, near Krakow. Will you help us?" He looked at us for a moment, and then motioned for us to follow him.

He let us into his house where we were given some hot milk and more soup. Then we were able to rest and enjoy our first moments of freedom.

"You'll have to move on soon," he said, "in case the Germans come back." His family gathered to stare at these strange shaven-headed creatures. "But for the moment, rest. Eat and rest."

The family who took us in, who helped us escape from that march of death, was of Polish-German stock, Germans whose ancestors had settled in Poland and intermarried into the local population generations ago. Enough Polish now to help us with the Germans, and enough German and Polish for me to feel I lived now only by the grace of the red triangle, rather than a yellow star on my jacket.

We rested up for a few days. Then they gave us some different old clothes, helped us remove the triangle patches from the dresses we kept on, gave us a few zlotys which we promised to return, and gave us directions to the railroad station.

Marysia and I walked off in that direction, everything felt unreal as if we were just pretending. Was this truly happening, were we free like other people, was it truly over? Had we actually survived?

We found the station and bought our tickets, third class tickets to the suburb of Krakow where Marysia's family, she believed, still lived. We had enough money, but just barely. People would stare at us in our rags with our sunken faces. We wore babushkas so as not to show our shaven heads, but we felt everyone knew anyway. Still everyone looked bad, now so close to the end of the war in the midst of the German retreat, that in fact, probably no one was paying much attention to us.

We soon arrived at the suburban station and made our way toward Marysia's house. She was shocked at the condition of the town, the craters where familiar buildings had been before. She told me that everything looked terrible, not at all as she remembered it. Then I looked at her, she looked slowly back at me, and we both laughed. We weren't looking so great ourselves just then.

When we reached her street, we saw that her family's house, thank God, was intact. We knocked on the front door. In a moment, a middle-aged woman opened it. It was Marysia's aunt, and the shriek of joy, of shock, echoed off the neighboring houses. We were taken in and smothered with love from the entire family.

Marysia's aunt kept us both well hidden for almost two weeks. The Germans were still in control in Krakow. They were being fought more openly now by Polish Partisans, but were still controlling the city. Her house had served as a cell and hideout for the Partisans during the war, even after Marysia's parents had fled, so we were all in constant jeopardy as long as the Germans remained in the city.

But soon enough they were gone, and the city was liberated by Russian troops. All those who had suffered under the Nazis for five years, the Partisans, the Jews, escaped camp inmates, common citizens, and all the rest emerged from hiding and began a celebration that would last for months.

Marysia's family brought out all the food they had or could scrounge, and fed us constantly. We spent most of our time in bed, being fed goodies. They gave us new dresses and burned our old camp clothes. We were pampered like princesses, a heady experience after Auschwitz.

Marysia told them that I had saved her life, that she had wanted many times to give up but I wouldn't let her. After they heard this, her family couldn't do enough for me.

Every day felt like a holiday. The two of us slept in the same bed, just like in the camp, but this time it was Marysia's bed upstairs, soft and plush and clean, without four other girls. We couldn't stop talking day and night about our experiences and escape. The family laughed at us, how we chattered long into the night.

"I could take a match and burn you," said Marysia's aunt. "You two would still not stop talking." It was a different world, like heaven, and we were enjoying it too much to sleep.

Only I was still Kazia to them, still a Polish girl to Marysia and her Polish family. The imprint was firm. To live, to survive, you must hide, dissemble, be clever and alert. You may feel happy, you may be clean, you may seem safe, but you never are. Always careful. If you want to live, you must keep the truth hidden.

Thus, I never told them who I was, never told them I was really a Jew. You never know. After all, a Jew had sent me to Auschwitz. With Poles, it was better to remain a Pole. You knew they hated the Germans, but you were never sure what they thought about the Jews.

After a few weeks' celebration with Marysia and her family, I finally told them that I had to check up on my own family. They lived in Hrubieszow, I told them, a distance of some 160 kilometers from Krakow. In the desolate aftermath of the war, telephones and mail were unreliable or nonexistent. To find out about my family, I would have to go and see. There was no other way to be sure. Marysia's aunt again urged me to stay, to wait and rest a while longer, and I did for a few more days, but soon I had to leave.

They asked me again to stay with them, to stay for good, but I couldn't. I had to know. Besides, I thought, I am still hidden, even here. They understood of course, at least what I told them, and they gave me enough money to take the train and bus to Hrubieszow.

Marysia and I swore to keep in contact, to meet again soon. We said our farewells with tears and heartbreak, but life was forcing separation on us, like shipwrecked sailors drifting apart on the open sea. Neither of us dreamed that we would ever meet again.

I had resolved in planning this trip that I would at long last establish contact with my beloved Marysia. My memory was faulty, but I had hoped that the sight of old scenes would jog it enough to release some useful clues. But not so.

In camp, we never used last names. Not us young ones anyway, and though I used to know Marysia's last name, I had forgotten it. (Did she remember Wisniewska?) I had also forgotten the family address. Neither of us dared to venture outside much, during those weeks when we were there together, so I'd never had to use it.

Jack and I thought of consulting official records, but without last names, how could the family be located? Without a street name and number, how could the house be pinpointed?

We were driven into the suburb where Marysia's family had lived and we wandered about, hoping I would recognize some street, some house, some landmark. But nothing. In fact, I'd hardly seen the outside of the house more than once or twice. Besides, this place had probably undergone as many big changes in the intervening years as everyplace else.

In despair, I wondered how this could possibly happen. We two had been so close, fellow sufferers, best friends, mutual helpers and supporters, confidants, partners in escape, literally bedfellows, and I couldn't remember something as basic as her last name and address.

In the end, we ran out of time, and had to return to our hotel in Warsaw. Urszula in Lublin and Marysia near Krakow, the two closest friends of my youth, had vanished from my life.

CHAPTER THIRTEEN

To Be A Jew

On the way back to Strzyzow, as in Marysia's house, as in the camp, as in Germany, as during every moment since the *Aktion* in Miaczyn, I never for a moment imagined that I would not find my parents, never for a moment dreamed that I was alone in the world. Despite what I saw every day in Auschwitz, I did not believe they were dead any more than I was. If I had believed that then, I would have let myself die.

On the train and bus, as I looked about the devastated land, the nightmares of my captivity came back, and I felt that surely things would now be different. The anger had been spent. From now on, no more wars, no more hatred, a better world. Even the stories about Warsaw, all but obliterated by the Nazis while the Russians waited just across the Vistula, and the sense of troubles to come with the occupying Red Army, did not discourage me. All that suffering must have been for something.

But then, as I looked about the train and bus, and at the villages we passed, that hope began slowly to fade The mutilated veterans, the mothers of children begging in the streets, the talk I overheard on the train about how terrible Jewish people are. It was no different from before. My God, I thought, was it all for nothing?

Then I thought, no, when we are together again, Mother

and Father and the girls and me, then we will be happy, alive, and free, and that will be the sense of it all.

When the bus arrived in Hrubieszow, I first sought out the other Jews who had been able to return to the town, or who had somehow escaped the ghetto and subsequent deportation. Not many were left, but I did run into somebody I knew, Miriam, the young Jewish girl I'd had to disavow in Auschwitz.

When we crossed paths, Miriam just stopped and stared at me. It took a moment, but then I walked up and hugged her.

"I was there as a Pole," I started to explain. "Didn't you see my red triangle?" She was naturally not too enthusiastic about meeting me, but she could see my side of it.

"Not then, but later I did," she answer stiffly. "And then I understood. It's all right," she added, softening. "I should have been more careful."

"I'm sorry," I said.

"For what? For God's grace? We're both alive. We all did what we had to do." We said no more and soon parted.

No one in Hrubieszow knew of my family. People I talked to were not encouraging. I began to hear strange new names. Majdanek, Sobibor, Treblinka. People who had been rounded up in the *Aktionen*, like that at Miaczyn, were sent to these places and rarely came back. Almost never, in fact.

A chill settled on my heart. I remembered that frightening moment along the roadside, the Einsatzgruppe, my dream of Mother. I could not help but put it together with what I had seen at Auschwitz. The women and children pushing and shoving to get to the gas chambers.

Oh God, Mother. Painfully, I tried to face the facts. Mother, Dora, and Grandmother had not been taken to a work camp as I had hoped, as I had pictured them all along, or they would not have been separated from us. They had probably been killed within hours of the *Aktion,* gassed as soon as they got to the camp, whichever camp. They were dead, all of them, *dead!* They had been dead for nearly three years.

Sick with despair, I tried to renew hope. There were miracles. Look at me. All the times I'd escaped. Perhaps. No! I pulled myself together. No more fantasies. I had to think of Father and David and Rivka.

Let's see, what had Father said. Yes, he would ask the good farmer, Jedgycz, for shelter and protection. Had Jedgycz taken them in? Everybody loved Father. Oh surely yes. Or if not Jedgycz, then certainly some other good man. There were many good men in Poland. (I blocked out memories of scrawlings on the walls, of fellow students wanting to "beat up some Jews," of peasants throwing stones at our trains thinking we were Jews.)

Surely even now, Father and David and Rivka were cautiously emerging from hiding, straightening up, looking about them.

The next day, I started to walk into Strzyzow along the familiar road I had traveled so many times before, on my journeys to and from school at Lublin.

As I neared the village, I slowed my pace and began to look about me. Everything seemed much the same. Yet I was afraid. What had they done to this region, the Germans, since the day they ordered us to leave everything and assemble in the town square.

I passed a Polish woman whom I recognized, and we both stopped. "Child," she said, "where are you going?" With effort, I recalled her name and used it, smiling at her.

"To Strzyzow," I said, wondering why it wasn't obvious to her, "to see if any of my family is there." Why would she ask?

"Moj Boze! My God, don't go there."

"Why not?"

"It is not safe for you. Last night they killed your old neighbor Bookstein and threw him into the Bug."

"Bookstein?" I echoed, stupefied. "The Germans killed Bookstein?" We had known him well. I had thought there were no Germans in that part of Poland any more.

"No," she said, humiliated, "not the Germans. The Poles." I might have known. It was still happening. A Jew came back to find his house and land occupied by a Pole. The Pole had gotten used to the idea that he owned the property and thought the land was his. All during the war, Jews were killed. Who would notice now? And if anybody knew, nobody would say much about it.

"Come, child," said the village woman. "Sleep over at my house, and in the morning, I will tell you what I know. You can go then if you still want to."

I had known this woman when I was a child and I trusted her, a good Polish woman, so I went to her house and slept greedily after my journey. There was plenty of time for the news—the rest of my life.

In the morning she gave me a large breakfast, cereal and hot milk, rolls, so good, so fresh. I had eaten well at Marysia's, but the hunger of Auschwitz was still unjustified. I ate quickly, knowing something bad was coming.

But finally, it was time for her to tell me what she knew. She waited until after the dishes were cleaned up. Then she sighed, "My child, you have no father, no brother, no sister any more."

"What do you mean? How do you know?" I felt my stomach turning. They were missing, maybe. They were someplace far away, Russia perhaps, but dead, so final?

"They killed them, my child."

"Who, the Germans?"

"Yes, someone told the Germans where they were hidden, so the Germans came and shot them."

"Who told them? Who?"

"Someone."

"From around here?"

"Yes, from around here."

"Polish?"

"Yes, of course. Polish."

The two of us, two women, one old and fat and gray, the other young and thin and growing strong and hard, both of us were in tears now. Blame didn't matter. Death mattered. So final. No hope.

"Come, my child," she said finally, "Come and I will show you where they are buried." We went out and walked toward a small field. In the damp soil she showed me a large mound. The grave, she said, of my father and brother and older sister. Isaac and David and Rivka.

Finally I was able to ask the last lingering question, "When?"

The old woman could hardly bring herself to answer. At last, throat working, she said, "Only three or four weeks before the Germans left." She pressed her hands to her face, and I saw the tears drip through her fingers. " Just before the Germans left." In a matter of days, they would have been safe. A matter of days.

And why? Not even for their land. Someone else had taken that already. No, just because they were Jews.

So I stood by that mound in the earth and thought. My mother is probably gone. Gassed. My father is dead in front of me. My baby brother and sister too. Another sister is with my mother, probably the first to die. I may never know. And Ida, my last sister, is gone, vanished, perhaps dead too. Why, for what?

Strzyzov, Poland, where I believe my father, sister, and brother are buried.

For being a Jew.

Being a Jew meant the taunts and teasing by other children when I was a child. It meant being called backward and unsophisticated and ignorant. For what? It meant having to fight for an education and losing out to those less qualified. It meant beatings and fear and discrimination everywhere.

And finally it had descended into this madness. Death, death for my family, death for the millions in the camps, death for me if I had not hidden my Jewishness.

I had survived. How? By hiding the fact that I was a Jew. By living a double life. By keeping those dangerous emotions, attitudes, identities locked away.

I looked at the kind, sorrowful face of the Polish woman who had brought me here and pressed her hand. Then I moved away. I had the feeling that Rosalia Orenstein had joined Isaac and David and Rivka in their unmarked grave. It was Kazia Wisniewska who strolled away.

There were soldiers everywhere, because the border was so near, but they made no attempt to halt our car. We must be getting close to Strzyzow, but I saw nothing I recognized. "This is it," the driver said.

Where were the little houses, the shops, the picket fences? What were these large bleak barrackslike buildings?

"They've made it a collective farm," the driver said casually. I suppose it was an old story to him. All over Poland little villages had become collective farms.

So this was Strzyzow now. It wasn't like coming home to my birthplace at all. I looked about, disoriented. Then suddenly I saw the sugar beet mill. That at least hadn't changed.

"Now I know where I am. Turn left here driver. It's not far away."

Once we reached that rough little field, I knew it immediately. I'd half-feared that something had been built over the sacred ground, but not so. Not out of respect for the dead but because it was too close to the border. Grass had grown over the raised spot that was the unmarked grave, but they were there. Jack and I got out of the car and stood at the graveside. Just the field, and in the middle of it, the lonely grave. A kind of paralysis seized me, and it was all I could do to put down the flowers we had brought.

Father and David and Rivka, I think, I'm glad they're together.

I glanced up and a few feet away some children were watching us. I must have been in some kind of shock, because I thought, it's them, my brother and sisters. My family. Still children and still alive!

I wanted to call out to them. It's me Rosalia. What are you standing there for? Aren't you going to come over and say hello?

Jack saw my face and was alarmed. "Rose, what's wrong?" He came over to hold me. Then whatever it was, it passed. No, these were just farm children.

They had been staring curiously at us. Now they began to speak. "Who are you? Why do you come here? Can we help you?" Very polite, very sweet.

I was myself again, breathing again. "Thank you," I said. "We're strangers here, just visiting. I thought I recognized someone, that's all."

On the drive home, we stopped in Hrubieszow for lunch. I enjoyed the good Polish food, soup, blintzes, pirogi, sour cream. Perhaps I had just been hungry back there at the graveside, and had turned faint for a moment.

When we emerged from the cafe after the meal, we found our car flanked by two police jeeps, and six or eight policemen checking it over.

The instant I saw them, a feeling of terror flared up in me. I was back, discovered, caught, trapped. "Now, we are lost," I said to Jack.

"Now, now, it's probably some technicality."

The police took our driver into one of the jeeps and began to question him. I heard him tell them that we were American Jews, coming to visit graves of relatives killed in the war. They listened noncommittally, then let him go and came over to us.

"Passports, please." We handed them over, and the police walked away with them. Jack tried to be reassuring, but I was too upset. Will they take us to jail now? Without our passports? Who could help us? Who would even know where we were? Finally the policeman returned.

"Why did you come here?" he demanded. I pulled myself together.

"I was born near here, in Strzyzow. You can see that on the passport. I came to see my family's grave. I haven't been back for almost 40 years, but before I die, I wanted to see that grave again." I broke down and began to cry.

Perhaps that was what convinced him that we weren't spies. As I was wiping my eyes, he handed me back the passports.

"I understand," he said. "And I have heard of this grave. I am sorry for you. Go home." He turned and signaled to the others. They let the driver go and moved their jeeps away from our car.

Leaving the home of the Polish peasant woman in Strzyzow, I traveled to Lodz, about 240 kilometers from Hrubieszow, a major city in central Poland, far away from my past. I'd never been there before. That's why I chose it.

There were Jews there, yes, Jews gathering from all over Poland, leaving the smaller towns where they no longer felt safe, clustering for protection and support in the major cities. Cousins of mine lived there, perhaps 15 minutes from where I settled, and when I first arrived, I visited them briefly. But after that I stayed away. I was Kazimiera Wisniewska again. I didn't want to be seen with them.

I kept thinking, feeling, I am not of them. I am not Orenstein. I gave that up years ago. But then who am I? Am I Wiszniewska, as in the camp? Am I Kukashuk, as in Germany? I do not know. I am no longer Rose. And I am no longer a Jew. That I do know.

And who was there to chide me? My mother? My father? My grandmother? They were all dead. They and 3,000,000 others, about 90 percent of Poland's Jews, had been wiped out. Jewish culture in Poland obliterated from the face of the earth. It was extinct. There was nobody any more to be faithful to.

And if I lived through all that as Kazimiera Wisniewska, then maybe that's who I really am. So I went to the Polish Relief Agency, and told them I was a refugee Polish girl, parents dead, family gone, no place to go. It was all true.

They helped me get a job and an apartment. My job involved bookkeeping and filing for an electrical supply company. Nothing difficult. Fairly pleasant.

The apartment was very nice too, completely furnished down to the last dish and spoon. Whoever had lived there before had moved out and left everything intact as we had done in Strzyzow in the *Aktion*.

They must have been middle-aged people. The taste of the furnishings said that. Old dark furniture, not fancy but clean. Red painted floors. Walls a light cream color. For me, it was heaven. My own home. Alone, clean, safe, nice. Mine.

But the past was still just below the surface. In the office one day, the subject turned to the Jews.

"You know," said one of my co-workers, "you can always tell a Jew. No matter what, you can always recognize them."

"What do you mean?" I answered slowly. "How do you

recognize them?" Inside, I went rigid, sick, with the old fear of discovery.

"Don't you?" asked the girl.

"I don't know. I don't know so many now." Oh God, I thought. *I don't know so many now.* What a thing to say.

"Look," the girl said, as if instructing a kindergarten class, "they talk different. They behave different. They dress different. They look different. They are a completely different breed." It was a flat irrefutable statement.

"Well," I said at last, "I can't really say. I don't really want to discuss it. I don't know them that well, and I don't think they're that different, but if you think so, it's fine with me."

The subject was changed then, but every time something happened that could be blamed on the Jews, the discussion was renewed. The Jews do this, the Jews do that, the Jews aren't like us. So, for me the war was not yet over. I was still hiding. Like in Auschwitz. Still playing a game. Still afraid.

Once, reading the paper, I saw the familiar name of "Mikolajczyk." He had come back from exile and was now Premier of the Polish government. Remembering his wife from the strickereien, I thought of our promises to meet again. I decided to go to Warsaw and speak to him, and to her if she was there.

I took the train, and was able to arrange a meeting with the Premier. He was very polite, but distant. His wife was still missing in the Auschwitz Death March, and the subject was clearly painful. I left, feeling empty.

Soon after, back in Lodz, I heard of an offer made through the Polish government to the many young people whose lives had been shattered by the war, an offer of free college education. I had not even finished high school, yet college had always been my dream. Education was hope, the future. Better than just sitting around wondering why I, among millions, had been chosen to survive. Better than the midnight thoughts of joining the 6,000,000 who did not.

But before I could apply, I would have to pass a high school equivalency examination. It had been six years since my last formal studies. I would need some tutoring.

One day I went shopping. What a pleasure it was to shop, to be able to buy food when you were hungry. There was a notice on a bulletin board posted by a girl who needed a room. I contacted her, and we met for coffee. It turned out that she had completed high school, and had even begun college just as the war broke out. So we made a deal. A free room for her, if she would tutor me for the equivalency exam.

This girl—I cannot even remember her name—was only two years older than I, but I used to think of her as an old maid. In terms of a normal life, I felt like a young girl. I'd never had the normal experiences of young womanhood. I knew suffering. I didn't know adulthood. My new roommate had lived the years denied to me, and I eagerly listened to all her life experiences.

She was a very neat, quiet woman. Something made me suspect that she too might have a secret. Perhaps it was that she too wanted to live inconspicuously in a room where she would not be noticed much. Was she Jewish herself? Had she guessed the truth about me? Fear probably kept both of us from ever saying anything. Best not to dig too deep. We were helping each other out. Did anything else really matter?

After a few months I took the exam and passed, excelling as before in math, and was accepted into the University in Lodz. I worked at my old job from 9:00 to 3:00, and then my boss gave me the rest of the afternoon off so I could study and attend classes. Sometimes I dreamed again of being a doctor, but biology and chemistry were given only during the day, so that was out of the question.

While I was at the University on a weekend field trip, I met Kazik. Count Kazik, in fact, although the "Count" part didn't matter much under a Communist regime. But I liked it anyway. It was kind of romantic. And so was he, in fact. Tall and blond and slim and polite, very refined. And very attractive.

We began to see a lot of each other. We had a great time together, moving in a good class of people, both at the University and among his friends. It was a life that I had never known before, except in books.

Clearly he came from a good family, and its position and wealth had survived the war more or less intact. He began to talk of introducing me to them. It was starting to get serious. I began to realize that I had fallen in love.

It had been so long since love was even a remote possibility that I hardly knew what I was feeling until many months had passed. Six or eight months perhaps. And all the time he was impeccably polite and never made any untoward advances. A true gentleman.

Soon I lay awake at night thinking about him. About how I really did love him and what that would mean. To marry him and live in Poland as a Pole, with a bright, good-looking husband, good family, what more could I want? I was living as a Pole anyway. Why not be a happy one? And rich didn't hurt, either.

But I had to know where I stood with him. Shouldn't he know who I really was? For a long time I considered confessing to him, but finally decided against it. It was not Rosalia he loved, it was Kazimiera. Still, he might find out some day.

Christmas came and went, and he was getting more and more serious, more and more intent. He wanted to ask his parents' approval for our engagement, but still I hesitated.

One night we were talking as usual, on the steps of my apartment building. I never let anybody up after dark, and he of course never asked.

"Let's talk to my parents this weekend. You know they'll say yes. They adore you, Kazia. They already think of you as their daughter."

"They are fine people, sweet people." I looked around the street, trying to find a way to say what I had to say.

"You know," I managed at last, "I don't see many Jews around here anymore." There, at last I'd said the word.

"No," he answered calmly, taking out a cigarette. "Not many, but still a few."

"Yes, a few still. But not like before." I drew my shawl tighter around myself.

"A lot before. Wherever you looked, you saw them." He lighted the cigarette and inhaled deeply. I'd always liked the smell of Turkish tobacco, and at first I paid more attention to the aroma than to what he was saying.

"Yes, Kazia," he went on, talking half to himself, musing. "You know, as good a job as Hitler did, he didn't do enough. But if I met a Jew today, some safe place, I would help finish the job. I would kill him with my bare hands." The words hung in the air like a physical presence. Unemotional. Calm. Almost polite. It was just how he felt, how he apparently had always felt. But for me it was worse than when the Gestapo came in Leverkusen. At least then I was half-expecting the worst.

Kazik's words came like the clammy hand of death in the dark. My whole body felt numb, paralyzed. As if my soul had just left it. At this very moment, I knew that my loyalty was to my family, and to myself. My Jewish destiny.

It is hard to remember what happened next. I know I managed to make my way upstairs. Did I say good night?

Good-bye? Anything? I don't know. Did he know what had happened? Probably not, although he may have reasoned it out later. I don't know or even care. I just knew I had to leave.

Leave it all. Leave this country. Leave this hiding.

That night in Lodz in 1946, after leaving Kazik, I packed a few clothes and some papers in a suitcase. When my roommate woke up the next morning, I was gone. Kazia had gone. I was returning to my heritage, to my people.

Epilogue

I ran away from Poland early in 1946, when it was still winter. After crossing the mountains, mostly at night, I reached Vienna. There, with the help of various Jewish organizations, I went to Germany, first to Munich and then to Lansberg. I stayed there for seven years, trying to find someone from my family, still hoping that some of them had managed to survive the horrors of the Holocaust.

There were many people like me at that time, living in camps organized especially for "displaced persons." I saw them trying desperately to start a new life. They fell in love, got married, and established families. Everybody wanted to forget, to go on living. I had nobody, and no place to go. I was even too tired to go to Palestine.

So I awaited my turn to leave for America. There were quotas, and the wait was long. Finally I reached New York in 1953. Not knowing much English, I found it difficult to find a job and support myself. But slowly I managed to learn keypunching, and started to work in an office on Wall Street.

Would I ever be able to forget? Unfortunately, there were things that didn't allow that to happen: the number from Auschwitz on my hand; people continually asking questions. Not everybody in America knew about death camp numbers at that time. They asked, "Is that your telephone number?" Hundreds of questions were repeated every day, in the office, on subways, in the street. I was young and attractive. Boys sometimes used the number on my hand to start a conversation that would lead to a date with me.

So I used to put a piece of Band-aid over the number. I wanted to hide it so that nobody would see it. I wanted to be like anybody else, without a number. Finally, in 1957, I had it surgically removed. It was no longer there to remind me of my past.

As the years went by, I decided to visit Israel. I did a lot of sightseeing, and visited all of my friends who had gone to live there. And it was in Israel that I met the man who was to become my husband.

Jack Toren worked as Chief Engineer of Transportation in Tel Aviv. I was supposed to leave in two or three days, but he wouldn't let me. Besides, I could not resist such an intelligent and handsome man. I fell in love, stayed in Israel, and we lived there for a year.

After a while, we moved to New York. I started to miss my friends and the cousins I had found in Europe who now lived in America. Life without family, which I had experienced in such painful measure, left me feeling very alone. The cousins I had found in Europe became my close family. Fred, Sam, and Henry Orenstein became my brothers, their wives, my sisters.

It was difficult in the beginning, but eventually we succeeded in organizing our life. We lived in Baltimore for one year, and my daughter was born there. In 1970, we moved to California.

I remained silent for 30 years. My memories were too painful, and I wanted to forget. Then in 1982 I started writing.

We all want to live. We all want to leave something behind. Good words, good memories. This true story is what I want to leave for my daughter. The understanding, the hope, and the lesson for young people never to give up. Always to go on, to try, to dream, to believe.

People say I'm lively. Yes, on the outside I am, but inside, I am alone. I want the pain to heal. Maybe it will, maybe not. Maybe.

In 1985, I decided to visit Poland, to see all the places again, to find the graves of my beloved family. I started this journey with a trembling heart. When I left Poland almost 40 years ago, I was a young woman. I went back in 1985 with my sad memories. Years before, I had left everybody behind in graves all over that country, and had run away over the mountains. Now I was returning as a mature woman filled with memories.

You may wonder, why did I go back there? What was I looking for? To torture myself? No, I wanted to tell the story. I wanted to tell the truth. All my life I had been like a sponge, taking everything in; now I wanted to squeeze it out. I wanted to leave my memories behind, but of course, in my heart, I will always remember.

Dramatis Personae

Grandmother, Mother, and My Youngest Sister, Dora
    Died in gas chamber in Sobibor in 1942.
Father, My Sister Rivka, and My Brother David
    Killed by Germans in Poland before the War
    Was Over In 1944.
Ida, My Sister
    Ran Away from Miaczyn in 1942.
    Have never heard from her.
My Cousin, Gary Herbst, Whose Father's Life I Saved
    Managed to survive the War. After the War,
    I met him in Hrubieszow.
    Later he left for America.